Financial
Derivatives market
and
its development in India

:: Author ::

Prakash Parmar

(M.Com., B.ed.,NET., M.B.A)

PUBLISHED BY

Chakravarti Siddharaj Jaysinh International
Publishing House
H.Q. At & Po. Chaveli., Ta- Chansma,
Dist- Patan, North Gujarat, India, Asia.
www.iphouseindia.com

First Publication: 8th December, 2014

Copyright: Author

(c) **Prakash Parmar**

ISBN:- 978-15-08473-01-5

Price: Rs.800/- INDIA

$ 15 OUTSIDE INDIA

PUBLISHED BY

Chakravarti Siddharaj Jaysinh International
Publishing House
HQ. At & Po. Chaveli., Ta- Chansma,
Dist- Patan, North Gujarat, India, Asia.
www.iphouseindia.com

Dedicated to my Loving Son Vraj

INDEX

INTRODUCTION

Stock exchanges have almost always remained as lucrative investment destinations in Indian context since their beginning. There have been many structural and policy changes in the Indian stock exchanges from time to time as per the requirement. The removal of erstwhile Carry Forward system matched by introduction of Derivative Trading on Indian bourses was an unprecedented phenomenon. Especially, post-derivatives, the Indian Stock Exchanges will never be same again. Various products in the F & O (Futures & Options) traded at the NSE and the BSE provide the market participants with an elbow room for taking positions in individual stocks as well as in indices. The stock markets the world over are highly volatile. Now, as the derivatives are here, the market participants can immunize themselves against such wild volatility making permutations and combinations of various positions in the futures and options.

However, it is not only the stock markets that have seen radical changes. Even the money and debt markets in India have seen sea changes thanks to the step of RBI permitting the introduction of Interest Rate Derivatives. The finance managers, or the Chief Financial Officers or more colloquially termed the bean-counters of India Inc., now have more sophisticated trading strategies for Interest Rate Risk Management which they were, hitherto, devoid of in the absence of any concrete measures on the part of the regulators. This change in the Indian Financial System will get them closer to their counterparts in the developed nations.

1

The reason for us to choose the subject of Derivative Trading is that the subject *per se* is complex enough to pose a great challenge to anyone working on it. For a layman, the subject is so complicated that trying to understand the nitty-gritty of the derivatives leaves him much confused. There are so many regulatory issues involved, risk containment measures, payoff charts, the trading strategies, valuation models *et al.* This is just a tip of the ice-berg. The subject itself is so wide that one can even go for a thesis on the subject that would qualify for a Ph.D.

In the pages that follow, we have made a humble effort to give justice to almost all the important issues involved in the derivatives. Section-1 deals with Futures & Options (F & O) segment of the capital markets, whereas Section-2 covers issues involving Interest Rate Swaps (IRSs) and Forward Rate Agreements (FRAs).

We hope that for the readers, this project-report would prove to be an authentic document on the subject to make reasonable conclusions and draw inferences from.

RESEARCH METHODOLOGY

(A) STUDY OBJECTIVES

❖ To study about derivatives market its participants and other various aspects of derivatives trading in the Indian context.

❖ To study about various types of hedging tools available In the Indian derivatives market.

❖ To study about different strategies used by market players to hedge the risk of their derivatives contracts.

2

❖ To study about the newly introduced derivative instruments in the Indian derivatives market like interest rate swaps, currency swaps and others.

(B) SCOPE OF THE STUDY

Scope of this project mainly defines the geographical and demographical region and its characterstics within which the studies have been undertaken.

The scope of my project is limited to Indian derivatives market and its various aspects. Here for the sake of convenience and data availability I decided to study in the Indian context only.

(C) METHOD OF DATA COLLECTION

The method of data collection I have implemented for my project is secondary method of data collection. As my project is a library project I did not go for any primary survey for the purpose of data collection, I have gathered the data with the help of many books and different websites.

(D) LIMITATIONS

❖ The scope of the project on study of the derivatives trading is limited to Indian context only so that certain aspects related to this market existing in foreign markets might not have been considered.

❖ The data that has been gathered for this project is made all the way through secondary sources so primary information related to investors and how do they actually try to hedge the price fluctuations of underlying assets might not have been reflected in the project.

Section-I
Futures & Options
Chapter 1
Financial Derivatives Market in India

FINANCIAL DERIVATIVES MARKET AND ITS DEVELOPMENT IN INDIA

Financial markets are, by nature, extremely volatile and hence the risk factor is an important concern for financial agents. To reduce this risk, the concept of derivatives comes into the picture.

Derivatives are products whose values are derived from one or more basic variables called basis. These bases can be underlying assets say: forex, equity, bases or reference rates.

For example, wheat farmers may wish to sell their harvest at a future date to eliminate the risk of a change in prices by that date. The transaction in this case would be the derivative, while the wheat would be the underlying asset.

Development of exchange-traded derivatives

Derivatives have probably been around for as long as people have been trading with one another. Forward contracting dates back at least to the 12th century and may well have been around before then. Merchants entered into contracts with one another for future delivery of specified amount of commodities at specified price.

A primary motivation for pre-arranging a buyer or seller for a stock of commodities in early forward contracts was to lessen the possibility that large swings would inhibit marketing the commodity after a harvest.

The need for a derivatives market

The derivatives market performs a number of economic functions:

1. They help in transferring risks from risk averse people to risk oriented people.
2. They help in the discovery of future as well as current prices.
3. They catalyze entrepreneurial activity.
4. They increase the volume traded in markets because of participation of risk averse people in greater numbers.
5. They increase savings and investment in the long run.

The participants in derivatives market

• Hedgers use futures or options markets to reduce or eliminate the risk associated with price of an asset.

• Speculators use futures and options contracts to get extra leverage in betting on future movements in the price of an asset. They can increase both the potential gains and potential losses by usage of derivatives in a speculative venture.

• Arbitrageurs are in business to take advantage of a discrepancy between prices in two different markets. If, for example, they see the futures price of an asset getting out of line with the cash price, they will take offsetting positions in the two markets to lock in a profit

Types of Derivatives

Forwards:

A forward contract is a customized contract between two entities, where settlement takes place on a specific date in the future at today's pre-agreed price.

Futures:

A futures contract is an agreement between two parties to buy or sell an asset at a certain time in the future at a certain price. Futures contracts are special types of forward contracts in the sense that the former are standardized exchange-traded contracts.

Options:

Options are of two types- calls and puts. Calls give the buyer the right but not the obligation to buy a given quantity of the underlying asset, at a given price on or before a given future date. Puts give the buyer the right, but not the obligation to sell a given quantity of the underlying asset at a given price on or before a given date.

Warrants:

Options generally have lives of up to one year, the majority of options traded on options exchanges have a maximum maturity of nine months. Longer-dated options are called warrants and are generally traded over-the-counter.

Leaps:

The acronym LEAPS means Long-Term Equity Anticipation Securities. These are options having a maturity of up to three years.

Baskets:

Basket options are options on portfolios of underlying assets. The underlying asset is usually a moving average or a basket of assets. Equity index options are a form of basket options.

Swaps:

Swaps are private agreements between two parties to exchange cash flows in the future according to a prearranged formula. They can be regarded as portfolios of forward contracts. The two commonly used swaps are:

- **Interest rate swaps:**

These entail swapping only the interest-related cash flows between the parties in the same currency.

- **Currency swaps:**

These entail swapping both principal and interest between the parties, with the cash flows in one direction being in a different currency than those in the opposite direction.

Swaptions:

Swaptions are options to buy or sell a swap that will become operative at an expiry of the options. Thus a swaption is an option on a forward swap, rather than having call and puts, the swaptions market has receiver swaptions and payer swaptions. A receiver swaption is an option to receive fixed and pay floating. A payer swaption is an option to pay fixed and receive floating.

Table 1 The global derivatives industry: Outstanding contracts, (in $ billion)

Table 23B: Derivative financial instruments traded on organised exchanges
By instrument and location
Number of contracts in millions

Instrument / location	Contracts outstanding				Turnover					
	Dec 2012	Dec 2013	Sep 2014	Dec 2014	2013	2014	Q1 2014	Q2 2014	Q3 2014	Q4 2014
Futures										
All markets	84.9	85.8	101.3	96.6	7,185.7	7,027.3	1,724.8	1,565.1	1,748.3	1,989.1
Interest rate	55.2	55.3	62.8	61.1	2,774.8	2,745.8	694.3	658.6	694.0	698.9
Currency	11.7	13.1	18.9	15.4	2,008.8	1,820.8	432.6	371.5	466.8	549.9
Equity index	18.1	17.4	19.6	20.1	2,402.1	2,460.8	598.0	535.0	587.5	740.3
North America	28.6	29.0	33.8	29.3	2,145.3	2,335.0	558.5	541.7	588.9	645.9
Interest rate	21.7	21.8	25.6	21.9	1,254.3	1,450.3	336.2	347.4	374.5	392.2
Currency	2.0	2.1	2.8	2.3	230.5	213.1	50.6	44.2	53.4	65.0
Equity index	4.9	3.1	3.5	5.1	660.6	671.7	171.7	150.1	161.1	188.8
Europe	22.5	23.2	26.6	24.2	2,207.6	2,353.2	615.2	504.1	552.4	681.5
Interest rate	11.6	12.0	12.6	11.9	919.8	783.0	225.3	200.3	180.8	176.6
Currency	3.3	3.5	5.4	3.8	476.6	729.3	172.2	117.8	169.4	269.9
Equity index	7.7	7.7	8.7	8.5	811.2	840.8	217.6	186.0	202.1	235.0
Asia and Pacific	10.7	8.7	11.3	12.4	2,147.5	1,692.0	381.3	380.1	434.4	496.2
Interest rate	2.4	2.8	3.1	3.4	164.3	164.5	38.2	38.2	42.5	45.6
Currency	3.5	1.9	3.5	3.4	1,139.4	687.5	157.5	165.4	195.8	168.8
Equity index	4.9	4.0	4.7	5.6	843.8	839.9	185.6	176.4	196.1	281.8
Other Markets	23.1	24.9	29.6	30.7	685.2	647.1	169.8	139.1	172.6	165.6
Interest rate	19.5	18.7	21.6	23.9	436.5	348.0	94.6	72.6	96.1	84.6
Currency	3.0	3.5	7.2	5.9	162.3	190.8	52.2	44.1	48.2	46.3
Equity index	0.6	0.6	0.9	0.8	86.5	108.3	23.0	22.4	28.2	34.7
Options										
All markets	125.8	123.2	149.5	127.0	3,889.9	4,105.0	936.5	829.3	1,055.9	1,283.3
Interest rate	53.5	50.1	58.7	50.3	565.5	565.9	155.9	140.4	143.1	126.6
Currency	3.7	3.7	6.5	8.0	403.9	248.7	50.2	34.8	57.8	105.9
Equity index	68.6	69.4	84.2	68.7	2,920.5	3,290.4	730.4	654.1	855.1	1,050.8
North America	32.4	44.2	60.1	51.6	781.2	936.2	231.6	212.0	232.1	260.4
Interest rate	12.1	20.3	32.5	28.6	286.5	365.3	87.2	84.9	96.6	96.6
Currency	0.5	0.7	1.0	0.8	15.4	17.3	3.7	3.2	5.0	5.4
Equity index	19.7	23.1	26.5	22.2	479.3	553.5	140.8	123.9	130.5	158.3
Europe	52.2	48.0	57.5	45.8	630.7	616.4	159.9	134.5	130.4	191.6
Interest rate	12.8	12.4	12.4	8.6	209.3	136.4	44.0	42.1	28.9	21.4
Currency	0.4	0.5	1.1	2.7	4.2	43.6	2.0	1.0	2.2	38.4
Equity index	39.0	35.1	44.0	34.5	417.2	436.4	113.8	91.4	99.4	131.8
Asia and Pacific	10.1	10.3	12.8	12.1	2,328.1	2,406.1	499.7	451.9	655.9	798.5
Interest rate	0.0	0.0	0.0	0.0	5.7	4.0	1.2	1.1	0.9	0.8
Currency	1.4	0.4	1.0	1.3	354.0	154.1	36.5	23.0	43.0	51.5
Equity index	8.6	9.9	11.8	10.8	1,968.4	2,248.0	462.0	427.9	612.0	746.2
Other Markets	31.1	20.8	19.1	17.5	149.9	146.4	45.3	30.9	37.4	32.8
Interest rate	28.5	17.4	13.8	13.2	63.9	60.2	23.4	12.3	16.7	7.7
Currency	1.3	2.1	3.4	3.1	30.4	33.7	8.0	7.6	7.5	10.6
Equity index	1.3	1.3	1.9	1.2	55.6	52.6	13.9	10.9	13.2	14.5

Factors driving the growth of financial derivatives

1. Increased volatility in asset prices in financial markets.
2. Increased integration of national financial markets with the international markets.
3. Marked improvement in communication facilities and sharp decline in their costs.
4. Development of more sophisticated risk management tools, providing economic agents a wider choice or risk management strategies, and
5. Innovations in the derivatives markets, which optimally combine the risks and returns over a large number of financial assets leading to higher returns, reduced risk as well as transactions costs as compared to individual financial assets.

Table 2 Turnover in derivatives contracts traded on exchanges

	Forwards, forex swaps and currency swaps	Options
Jun 2000	423	507
Dec 2000	423	528
Jun 2001	416	546
Dec 2001	471	564
Jun 2002	427	518
Dec 2002	434	503
Jun 2003	438	498
Dec 2003	429	605
Jun 2004	442	560
Dec 2004	448	611
Jun 2005	440	591
Dec 2005	464	624
Jun 2006	475	606
Dec 2006	481	567
Jun 2007	486	558
Dec 2007	497	570
Jun 2008	496	636
Dec 2008	515	641
Jun 2009	556	640
Dec 2009	570	628
Jun 2010	565	654
Dec 2010	570	635
Jun 2011	551	648
Dec 2011	485	651
Jun 2012	487	689
Dec 2012	527	872
Jun 2013	496	902
Dec 2013	472	728
Jun 2014	462	719

Chapter 2
History of F & O
FUTURES- THE HISTORICAL BACKGROUND

Futures contracts on commodities have been traded for long. In the USA, for instances, such contracts began trading on the CBOT in the 1860s. However, in the past three decades, financial futures contracts have been evolved.

The financial futures, probably, are a very significant financial innovation. They encompass a variety of underlying assets-securities, stock indices, interest rates and so on. The beginnings of financial futures were made with the introduction of currency futures contracts on the International Monetary Markets (IMM) - a division of the Chicago Mercantile Exchange (CME) - in May 1972.

Subsequently, interest rates futures- where the contract is on an asset whose price is dependent solely on the level of interest rates- were introduced on the CBOT in October 1975. Within a short span of time, CBOT made a headway and introduced the Government National Mortgage Association Contract (GNMA), and years 1976 and 1977 saw the launching by IMM, respectively, of 'the treasury bill futures' and 'treasury bond futures'.

A futures contract in treasury bonds is one of the most actively traded futures contract in the world and it has, in particular, lent great impetus to the introduction of similar futures on many futures exchanges the world over. The 'Eurodollar time deposit' futures contract (the Eurodollar is a dollar deposited in an American or foreign bank outside the

USA), which started trading on the IMM in December 1981, was the first contract that was settled in Cash, involving no delivery of the underlying asset.

An important development took place in the world of futures contracts in 1982 when stock index futures were introduced in the USA. Although some futures contracts on indices were traded in Europe in the 1970s; however, trading could not mature, as it was mainly done outside the exchanges.

It was in America only that a formal beginning was made when the Kansas City Board of Trade (KCBT) introduced stock index futures contracts with the 'value line index' serving as the underlying index. In the mean time, the CME tied up with S&P. In the August 1983, the CBOT developed its own stock index contract.

A futures contract on a stock index has been a revolutionary and novel idea because it represents a contract based *not* on a readily deliverable physical commodity or currency or other negotiable instrument.

It is instead based on the concept of a mathematically measurable index that is determined by the market movement of a predetermined set of equity stocks.

OPTIONS- THE HISTORICAL BACKGROUND

The concept of options is not a new one. In fact, options have been in use for centuries. The idea of an option existed in ancient Greece and Rome. The Romans wrote options on the cargoes that were transported by their ships. In the 17th century, there was an active options market in Holland. In fact, options were used in a large measure in the 'tulip bulb mania' of that century.

However, in the absence of mechanism to guarantee the performance of the contract, the refusal of many put option writers to take delivery of the tulip bulbs and pay the high prices of the bulbs they had originally agreed to, led to bursting of the bulb bubble during the winter of 1637. A number of speculators were wiped out in the process.

Options were traded in the USA and UK during the 19th century but were mainly confined to the agricultural commodities. Earlier, they were declared illegal in the UK in 1733 and remained so until the Act declaring them illegal was repealed.

They were again banned in the third decade of this century, albeit temporarily. In the USA, options on equity stocks of the companies were available on the OTC market only, until April 1973. They were not standardized and involved the intra-party risk.

In India, options on stocks of companies, though illegal then, had been traded for many years, in a limited form. As such, this trading has been a very risky proposition to undertake.

In spite of the long time that has elapsed since the inception of options, they were, until not very long ago, looked down upon as mere speculative tools and associated with corrupt practices.

Things changed dramatically in the 1970s when options were transformed from relative obscurity to a systematically traded asset which is an integral part of financial portfolios.

The year 1973 witnessed some major developments. Black and Scholes published a seminal paper explaining the basic principles of options pricing and hedging. In the same year, the Chicago Board of Options Exchange (CBOE) was created. It was first registered securities exchange dedicated to options trading. While trading in options existed for long, it experienced a gigantic growth with the creation of this exchange. The listing of options meant orderly and thicker markets for this kind of securities. Options' trading is now undertaken widely in many countries besides the USA and UK. In fact, options have become an integral part of the large and developed financial markets.

With full-fledge market for options trading here in India, the growth of the futures and options markets is unending.

Chapter 3
Advantages of Derivatives

ADVANTAGES OF DERIVATIVES

From an investor's point of view, derivatives offer a huge number of opportunities, whether he is risk-taker or risk averse. Derivatives, especially index futures and stock options, through their 'n' number of permutations and combinations, provide a great many number of trading strategies for the investors elaborated elsewhere the main advantages to an investor flowing from *smart* use of various derivative instruments are as discussed below:

- **Power to leverage:**

Derivatives allow investor to take position of a large value by making a small investment.

In futures, one takes a position by paying a margin in the range of 25-30%. In case of an option, one pays a premium that is a very small amount relative to the spot price and takes position in the markets.

For example, Call Option of Satyam Computers with a strike price of Rs. 220, expiring October, is available at Rs. 5. The market lot of Satyam is 1200. This means by investing Rs. 6000 one can take a position of a contract valued at Rs. 2,64,000.

- **Power to defer:**

The cash markets have a daily settlement mechanism. A speculator wanting to take a position in a stock has to either take delivery or square off his position the same day. Thus he is unable to take a position beyond a day.

With futures, one can take a position on a stock today, while the settlement takes place at a Future date. In this aspect, Futures are similar to the erstwhile Badla system as it enables carry forward of positions.

- **Power to lend or borrow from the markets:**

With futures, one can lend or borrow funds from the market. This will become more effective when actual deliveries are introduced in the derivatives markets.

In case you need money for short-term requirements, you can sell your stocks in the cash market and buy Futures. You get the liquidity for some time and then you can get your stock back when the futures are settled.

However, this is a profitable ***only when*** the particular stock's futures price is less than its theoretical price as given by "Net Cost to Carry Model".

For example, spot price of Satyam is Rs. 200. Satyam one-month futures are quoting at Rs. 205. If one has funds, one can buy Satyam in spot market and sell it in Futures market. Effectively, one has lent Rs. 200 to the market and earned an interest of Rs. 5 for a one-month period.

Chapter 4
Benefits of Derivatives To Indian Capital Markets

BENEFITS OF DERIVATIVES TO INDIAN CAPITAL MARKETS

India's financial market system will strongly benefit from smoothly functioning index derivatives markets. The reasons in support of this statement are as follow: -

• Internationally, the launch of derivatives has been associated with substantial improvements in market quality on the underlying equity market. Liquidity and market efficiency on India's equity market will improve once the derivatives commence trading.

• Many risks in the financial markets can be eliminated by diversification. Index derivatives are special insofar as they can be used by investors to protect themselves from the one risk in the equity market that cannot be diversified away, i.e. a fall in the market index. Once investors use index derivatives, they will suffer less when fluctuations in the market index take place.

• Foreign investors coming into India would be more comfortable if the hedging vehicles routinely used by them worldwide are available to them. So, the foreign funds inflow through FIIs in Indian capital markets will be more making it easier for the corporate to tap the funds at a cheaper rate.

• The launch of derivatives is a logical next step in the development of human capital in India. Skills in the financial sector have grown tremendously in the last few years, thanks to the structural changes in the market, and the economy is now ripe for derivatives as the next area for addition of skills.

The launch of futures trading has been a milestone on Indian bourses although its full impact is yet not visible due to certain roadblocks. As the markets are becoming more volatile and complex, there is a need to hedge these risks and hence for instruments, which allow fund managers to manage risk, better.

As our Indian market lacks infrastructure available, therefore our futures market is not perfect as it must be. For example, as we lack a system of electronic fund transfer in the banking sector and we don't even have the short term yield curve which can be used to calculate the fair price for the index future. As market becomes deep, the need for these deficiencies to go will be stronger.

If the penetration of the equity cult among investors is any indication, we have a large investor population, one among the largest in the world. The Indian markets lack the kind of institutional presence, which is available in the developed countries, but now that too is becoming a matter of history.

As our market is on retail basis therefore we require great protection against counter-party risk. It is the regulators that have nurtured the entire derivatives initiative and have played a very positive role. They may extend the support, guidance and advice while derivatives have been introduced. Even the regulatory framework, which has been designed, puts the Indian derivatives market best in the world.

However, volumes in derivatives markets are still too small to have its comparison with developed countries' capital markets. The derivatives market, which gives better price discovery, can have a positive impact on the cash market. It would increase the liquidity even in the cash market where arbitrage takes place between the futures and the cash market.

Although introduction of derivatives implies better risk management and deeper market, we cannot mean that volatility decreases, as volatility is the growing phenomenon. Volatility in other instruments like interest rates, equities or foreign exchange has increased as compared to past levels. That is something, which we have to live with.

Here, derivatives would no doubt increase the liquidity and depth. Within index futures Indian bourses would be launching sectoral index futures like Infotech or FMCG index. Among other products, we would like to bring futures on foreign exchange and fixed income instruments.

So, in a nut-shell, the Indian capital markets, with the full-fledged derivatives market will never be the same as it used to be.

Chapter 5
Market Participants in F & O Market
MARKET PARTICIPANTS IN F & O MARKET

The derivative instruments are used for various purposes. As indicated earlier, they are primarily used for purposes of managing risk by those managing funds.

The trading of these instruments also allows the market participants the opportunities of making profits either by taking risk, i.e*., **speculation**, or simultaneously taking opposite positions in the spot and futures market, or in the futures markets alone, to take advantage of price differentials, i.e., **arbitrage.**

Accordingly, there are varied types of traders who trade in the futures and options markets. Hedgers, speculators, and arbitrageurs constitute three major classes of such traders.

1)   Hedgers:

As already observed, hedging (covering against losses) is the prime reason which led to emergence of derivatives. The availability of derivatives allows the undertaking of many activities at a substantially lower risk. Hedgers, therefore, are an important constituent of the traders in the derivatives markets.

Hedgers are the traders who want to eliminate the risk (of price change) to which they are already exposed. They may take a long position on, or short sell, a commodity and would, therefore, stand to lose should the prices move in the adverse direction. It will be instructive to illustrate hedging with some examples.

To begin with, suppose a leading trader buys a large quantity of wheat that would take two weeks to reach him. Now, he fears that the wheat prices may fall in the coming two weeks and so wheat may have to be sold at lower prices. The trader can sell futures (or forward) contracts with matching price, to hedge.

Thus, if wheat prices do fall, the trader would lose money on the inventory of wheat but will profit from the futures contract, which would balance the loss.

Again, traders dealing in exports and imports are subject to fluctuations in the foreign exchange rates, called the *forex risk*. In the absence of any hedging instruments, they are bound to remain exposed to such risk and suffer in case of adverse changes in the exchange rates. However, the forex risk, an integral component of the foreign trade business, can be hedged with derivatives. For example, today, with the dollar-rupee forward contracts and with cross-currency options in India, it is possible to engage in foreign trade with a lesser degree of risk.

As another example, consider a fund manager who believes in stock picking. However, at the same time, he has to live with the real risk that his analysis of securities may go awry. In such situations, the stock index derivatives may be employed in order to eliminate/ reduce the risk.

It may be noted that hedging only makes an outcome more certain, it does not necessarily lead to an improved outcome. Suppose, today's dollar-rupee exchange rate is US $1 = Rs. 47.50, while the three-month forward rate is US $1 = Rs.

48.40. Suppose, an Indian firm has a commitment to pay $ 100,000, three months from now. The firm, being unsure of the way the dollar-rupee exchange rate would move in the three months' time, decides to buy a forward contract and lock in the exchange rate. It involves no initial payment. With this, the firm knows for sure that it would need Rs. 48,40,000 to meet its obligation. Now, at the end of three months, if the rate becomes $1 = Rs. 49.20, then the firm would stand to gain Rs. 80,000. Without, the forward contract, the payment needed would have been Rs. 49,20,000. Similarly, if the exchange rate were $1 = Rs. 48.10, then the firm would regret having entered into forward contract, because it would have to pay Rs. 48,40,000 for something that could be bought for Rs. 48,10,000, without the contract.

Of course, the firm may alternatively consider hedging through buying an options contract also. It would enable the firm to avoid the loss involved in buying US dollars if they become cheaper in terms of Indian rupees, and enjoy the profit if the movement in the exchange rate were favorable.

Nevertheless, while a forward contract requires no payment, an options contract involves an initial cost: if the call is not exercised, the premium paid for it becomes a net loss while if it is exercised, the profit resulting from the call exercise would be reduced by this cost.

2)   Speculators:

If hedgers are the people who wish to avoid the price risk, speculators are those who are willing to take such risk. These are the people who take positions in the market and assume risks to profit from fluctuations in prices.

In fact, the speculators consume information, make forecasts about the prices and put their money in these forecasts. In this process, they feed information into prices and thus contribute to market efficiency.

By taking positions, they are betting that a price would go up or they are betting that it would go down. Depending on their perceptions, they may take long or short positions on futures and/or options, or may hold spread positions (simultaneous long and short positions on the same derivative).

In the absence of the derivatives, speculation activity would become very difficult as it might require huge funds to be invested. For example, if an investor believes that the price of a share is likely to rise substantially, then he would need a very large sum of money to buy the shares, keep them and sell them off when the price rises.

With derivatives, however, it is much easier to do so because the derivatives are highly levered instruments. If the speculator's prediction of direction and amount of price change is correct, huge profits can be realized. For example, suppose that a share is currently quoted at Rs. 32 and a speculator is strong on this share.

Assume that a call option, with exercise price of Rs. 35 and due in one month, on this share is available in the market at 50 paise (per share).

Buying this option would require Rs. 50 (a call is for 100 shares) only. Now, if the price of the share is either less than, or equal to, Rs. 35, the call shall not be exercised and the loss would be Rs. 50 or 100% of the investment.

If, on the other hand, the price rules at Rs. 40, then a gain of 100*(Rs. 40-Rs. 35) = Rs. 500 would be made, which works out to be 900% of the investment! With no option or other derivative available, the investor would be required to invest Rs. 3200 (for 100 shares) and would make a profit of Rs. 800 i.e. only 24% of the amount invested.

Not only that, much bigger losses would be incurred if the share price were to settle at less than Rs. 32. Obviously, therefore, the derivatives adequately address the needs of the speculators without threatening the market integrity in the process.

The speculators in the derivatives markets may either be **day traders or position traders.** The day traders speculate on the price movements during one trading day, open and close positions many times a day and do not carry any position at the end of the day.

Obviously, they monitor the prices continuously and generally attempt to make profit from just a few ticks per trade. On the other hand, the position traders also attempt to gain from price fluctuations but they keep their positions for longer durations-may be for a few days, weeks or even months.

They use fundamental analysis and/or technical analysis as also any other information available to them to form their opinions on the likely price movements.

3)   Arbitrageurs:

Arbitrageurs thrive on market imperfections. An arbitrageur profits by trading a given commodity, or other item, that sells for different prices in different markets. The definition of arbitrage can be given in this manner:

"Simultaneous purchase of securities in one market where the price thereof is low and sale thereof in another market, where the price thereof is comparatively higher.

These are done when the same securities are being quoted at different prices in the two markets, with a view to make a profit and carried on with the conceived intention to derive advantage from difference in prices of securities prevailing in the two markets."

Thus, arbitrage involves making risk-less profit by simultaneously entering into transactions in two or more markets. If a certain share is quoted at a lower rate on the Delhi Stock Exchange (DSE) and at a higher rate on the Ahmedabad Stock Exchange (ASE), for example, then arbitrageur would profit by buying the share at DSE and selling it at ASE.

This type of arbitrage is arbitrage over 'space'. With the introduction of derivatives trading, the scope of arbitrageurs' activities extends to arbitrage over 'time'.

For instance, if an arbitrageur feels that the futures are being quoted at a high level-considering the cost of carry-he could buy securities underlying an index today and sell the futures, maturing in a month or two hence.

Similarly, since futures and options with various expiration dates are traded in the market, there are likely to be several arbitrage opportunities in trading.

Thus, if a trader believes that the price differential between the futures contracts on the same underlying asset with differing maturities is more or less than what he/she perceives them to be, then appropriate positions, in them, may be taken to make profits.

The existence of well-functioning derivatives markets alters the flow of information into the prices. This is because in a purely cash market, speculators, feed information into the sport prices. In contrast, the presence of a derivatives market, besides a cash market, ensures that a major part of the transformation of information into prices takes place at the derivatives market, due to lower transaction costs involved in such a market, and then it gets transmitted to the spot markets. It is here that the arbitrageurs provide a link between the derivatives market and the cash market by synchronizing the prices in the two. Thus, through their actions, the arbitrageurs provide a critical link between the cash and derivatives markets.

Chapter 6
Payoff Profile of F & O

PAY-OFF PROFILE OF F&O

Payoff profile for a buyer of Futures:

The payoff profile for Futures is linear. As the spot price increases, the profit from **having bought** a Future increases. Similarly, as spot price decreases, the profit from **having sold** Futures increases and is a mirror image of the profit from buying. The point where the spot price and the Futures price are same is the breakeven point.

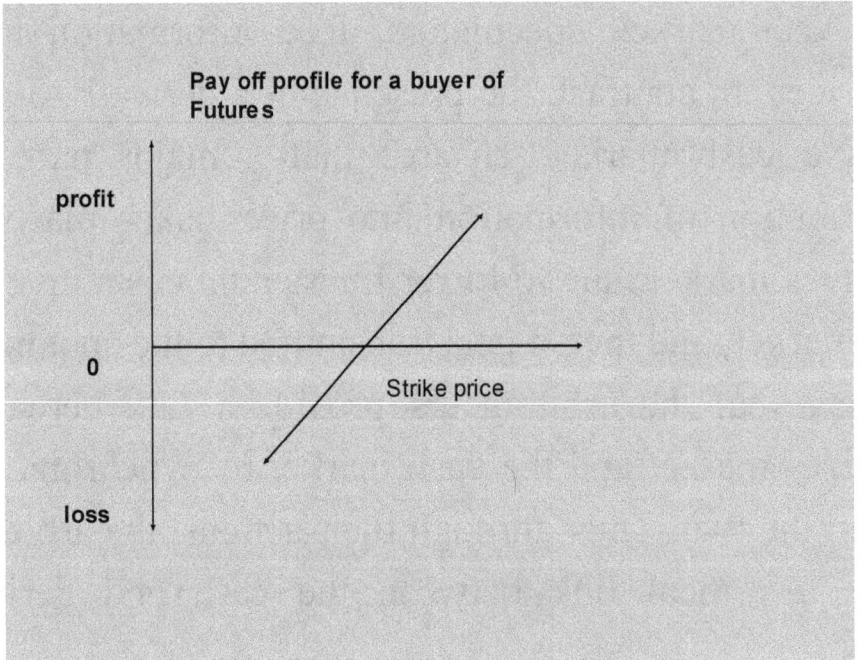

Payoff profile for a buyer of Call Options:

In Options, in case of a call, it is an Option to buy an asset at strike price. The maximum profit for the buyer of a Call Option is theoretically unlimited and maximum loss is limited to the extent of Option premium.

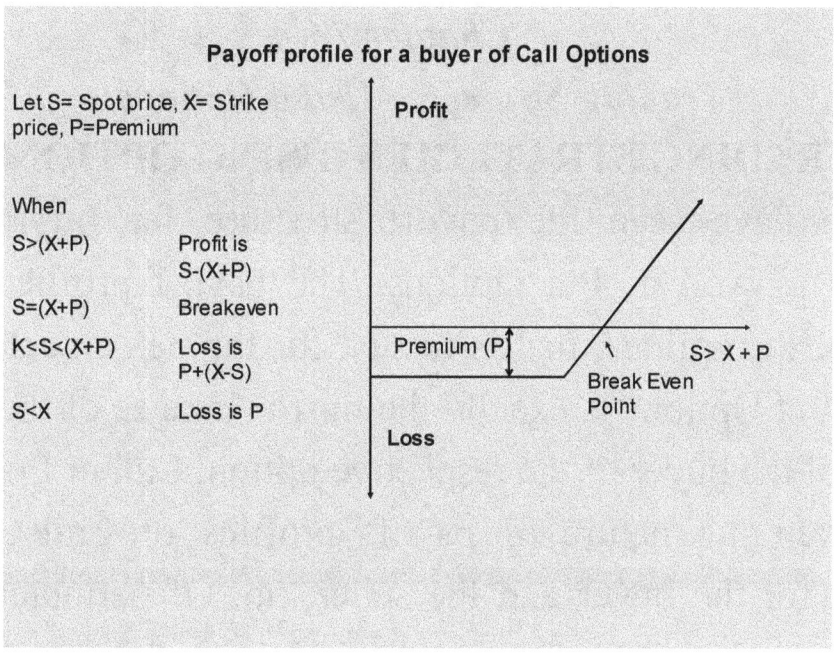

Payoff profile for a buyer of Put Options:

Put Option is an Option to sell an asset at the strike price. As with any long position, the loss is limited to the premium paid with an unlimited potential for profit. However, since spot prices cannot be negative, the unlimited gain would be limited to X, the strike price, since the maximum gain can be X when the spot price touches zero.

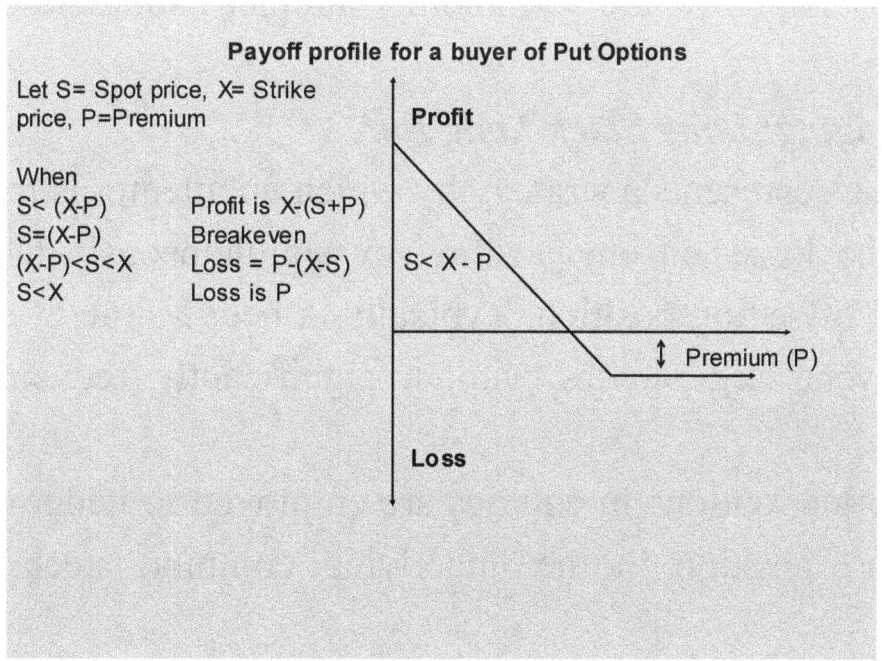

Chapter 7
Trading Strategies-Using Options
TRADING STRATEGIES -USING OPTIONS

We have seen the payoff structure for **buying** Call Options as well as Put Options. The payoff profile for the writer of the options, that is to say, for the person **selling** the Call or Put Options is exactly the mirror images of the payoff profile of the buyer of the respective option, Call or Put.

Given the nature of payoff profiles of Call and Put Options for the buyer and the seller, no. Of permutations as well as combinations can be thought of involving Options, Futures (with same or different Exercise Prices) as well as underlying asset (that is to say, individual stock).

The strategy being employed by an investor amply underlies his attitude towards risk-whether he is risk averse or risk taker, his expectation about future prices-whether he is bullish on the market or bearish. In the coming pages, we present some of the commonly adopted strategies using options.

(1) Hedging: Long Stock Long Put

Hedging represents a strategy by which an attempt is made to limit the losses in one position by simultaneously taking a second offsetting position. Typically, a hedge strategy strives to prevent large losses without significantly reducing the gains.

Very often, options in equities are employed to hedge a long or short position in the underlying common stock. Such options are called covered options in contrast to the uncovered or naked options, discussed earlier.

This strategy viz. Long Stock Long Put involves buying a stock and simultaneously buying a Put Option.

An example will demystify the nitty-gritty.

Consider an investor who buys a share for Rs 100. To guard against the risk of loss from a fall in its price, he buys a put for Rs 16 for an exercise price of, say, Rs 110. He would, obviously exercise the option only if the price of the share were to be less than Rs. 110. The following table gives the profit/ loss for some selected values of the share price on maturity of the option.

Share Price	Exercise Price	Profit on exercise (i)	Profit/ loss on share held (ii)	Net Profit (i) + (ii)
70	110	24	-30	-6
80	110	14	-20	-6
90	110	4	-10	-6
100	110	-6	0	-6
110	110	-16	10	-6
120	110	-16	20	4
130	110	-16	30	14
140	110	-16	40	24

For instance, at a share price of Rs. 80, the put will be exercised and the resulting profit would be Rs. 14, equal to Rs. 110 – Rs. 80, or Rs. 30 *minus* the put premium of Rs. 16.

With a loss of Rs. 20 incurred for the reason of holding the share, the net loss equals to Rs. 6.

The profits resulting from the strategy of holding a long position in the stock and long put are shown in the following figure. In all the figures that follow now, the dashed lines depict the relationship between the profit and stock prices for the stock in question, on the one hand, and profit and the option on the other hand. The solid line in each case depicts the relationship between profit and stock prices **for the whole portfolio.** It may further be noted that the profit/ loss shown is on a per share basis.

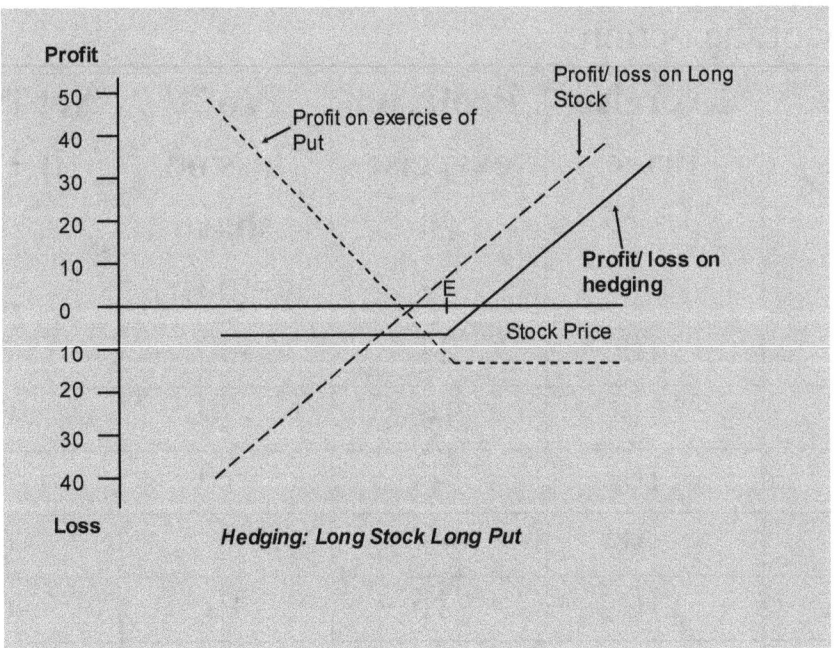

Hedging: Long Stock Long Put

(2) Hedging: Short Stock Long Call

Unlike an investor with a ling position in stock, a short seller of stock anticipates a decline in stock prices. By shorting the stock now and buying it at a later date at a lower price in the future, the investor intends to make a profit.

Any price increase can bring losses because of an obligation to purchase at a later date. To minimize the risk involved, the investor can buy a call option with an exercise price equal to or close to the selling price of the stock.

Let us take a hypothetical case of an investor who shorts a share at Rs. 100 and buys a call option for Rs. 4 with a strike price of Rs. 105. The conditional payoffs resulting from some selected prices of the share are shown in the next table.

Share Price	Exercise Price	Profit on exercise (i)	Profit/ loss on share held (ii)	Net Profit (i) + (ii)
90	105	-4	15	11
95	105	-4	10	6
100	105	-4	5	1
105	105	-4	0	-4
110	105	1	-5	-4
115	105	6	-10	-4
120	105	11	-15	-4

The following figure illustrates the strategy.

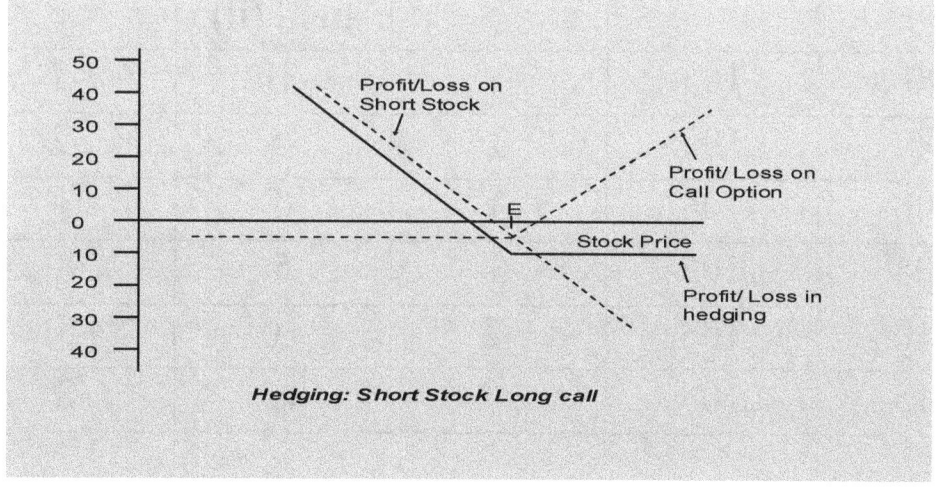

Hedging: Short Stock Long call

(3) Hedging: Long Stock Short Call

In the previous two strategies, the investor takes *Long* positions in the Option- be it Call or Put. Hedging can also be undertaken by writing (*taking a Short position*) Call as well as Put Options in appropriate circumstances.

One of such strategies is to *write* a covered call option when the investor has already taken a long position in the underlying individual stock. If the common stock is not expected to witness a significant change, either way, in the near future, then the strategies of writing calls and puts may be usefully employed to minimize the risk. The following paragraph shows-How?

Take for an example, if an investor has bought a share for Rs. 100, he can employ this strategy by writing a call option with the strike price of, say Rs. 105, with the premium of Rs. 3. The profit/ loss occurring at some prices of the underlying share, is indicated in the following table.

Share Price	Exercise Price	Profit on exercise (i)	Profit/ loss on share held (ii)	Net Profit (i) + (ii)
90	105	3	-10	-7
95	105	3	-5	-2
100	105	3	0	3
105	105	3	5	8
110	105	-2	10	8
115	105	-7	15	8

| 120 | 105 | -12 | 20 | 8 |

The following chart explains the same phenomena graphically.

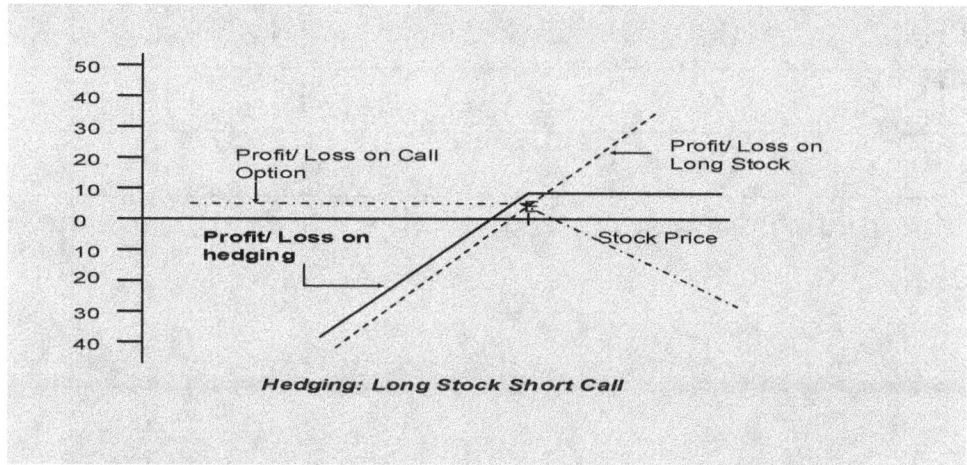

Hedging: Long Stock Short Call

(4) Hedging: Short Stock Short Put

Exactly adverse strategy is to be adopted when the investor short sells the share. He can hedge by writing a Put Option. Thus, by undertaking 'to be a buyer', the investor hopes to reduce the magnitude of loss that would be from an increase in the stock price, by limiting the profit that could be made when the stock price declines.

Suppose, an investor shorts a share at Rs. 100 and write a put option for Rs.3, having an exercise price of Rs. 100. Clearly, the buyer of the put will exercise the option only if the share price does not exceed the exercise price. The table giving conditional payoff is given below:

Share Price	Exercise Price	Profit on exercise (i)	Profit/ loss on share held (ii)	Net Profit (i) + (ii)
90	100	-7	10	3

95	100	-2	5	3
100	100	3	0	3
105	100	3	-5	-2
110	100	3	-10	-7
115	100	3	-15	-12
120	100	3	-20	-17

For the pictorial presentation of this strategy, see the next page.

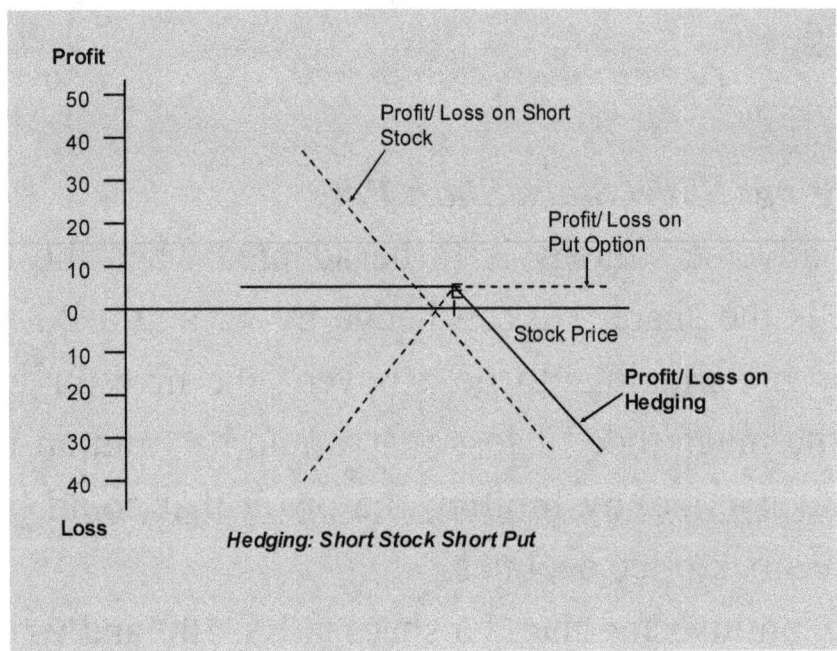

Hedging: Short Stock Short Put

(5) Bull Spread Using Calls

Spread trading strategy involves taking a position in two or more options of the same type.

This strategy viz. Bull Spread is undertaken when one is bullish about the future price movements in the stock prices. However, Bull Spread can be affected using Calls as well as Puts. The latter is explained in the next head of strategy.

This strategy calls for buying a Call Option on a stock and writing the Call Option on the same stock with the same maturity date, but with a higher exercise price. It may be noted that in case of Call Options, premium on the Option with lower exercise price is greater than that on Option with higher exercise price.

So, in a way, this strategy involves some initial cost as the premium receivable for writing a Call Option (with a higher exercise price) would be less than the premium payable on the Call Option bought (with a lower exercise price).

If on the expiry, the stock price is less than the lower exercise price, both the Call Options would be Out-of-money and, hence, both would expire unexercised. In that case, net outflow would be initial cost as represented by the difference between the premium payable (which is higher) and premium receivable.

If on the expiry, the stock price lies between the two exercise prices, then the Call with the lower exercise price (which the investor has bought) would be exercised and the Call with the higher exercise price (which the investor has sold) would expire unexercised. So, the net profit would be the difference between the stock price and the exercise price of bought option *minus* the initial spread cost, as represented by the difference between the premium payable and the premium receivable.

If the last possibility i.e. the stock price being greater than the higher exercise price, happens, then, both the Call Options, being in-the-money, would be exercised. The resultant net profit would be the difference between the two exercise prices as reduced by the initial spread cost, as represented by the difference between the premium payable and the premium receivable.

The payoff table for the Bull Spread (Using Calls) is as shown below:

Price of Stock	Payoff from Long Call	Payoff from Short Call	Total Payoff
$S_1 >= E_2$	$S_1 - E_1$	$E_2 - S_1$	$E_2 - E_1$
$E_1 < S_1 < E_2$	$S_1 - E_1$	O (Not Exercised)	$S_1 - E_1$
$S_1 <= E_1$	O (Not Exercised)	O (Not Exercised)	0

The corresponding graphical presentation is as shown under:

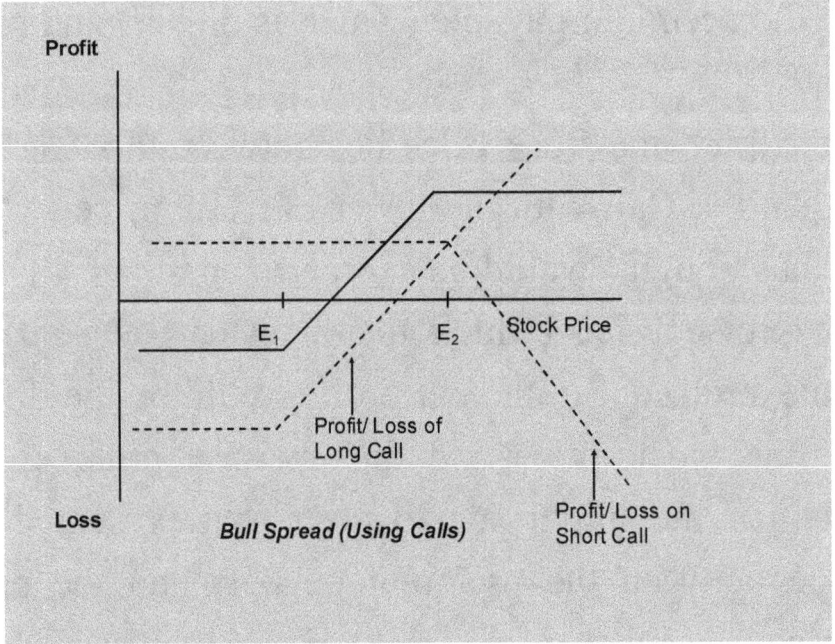

Bull Spread (Using Calls)

(6) Bull Spread Using Puts

In this strategy, the investor purchases a Put Option on the underlying and writes a Put Option on the same underlying and with the same expiry date, but with a higher exercise price. Here also, there would be a difference between the premiums payable and premium receivable. The premium payable on the bought Put Option (with a lower exercise price) would be less as compared to the premium receivable on the sold Put Option (with a higher exercise price).

Now, suppose, on the expiry, the price of the underlying is less than the lower exercise price, then both the Put Options would be exercised. The net result would be the difference between premium received and premium paid *minus* the loss on exercise prices of the two options (as represented by the difference between the two exercise prices).

If, on the expiry, the price of the underlying is between the two exercise prices, then the Put Option with higher exercise price (which was sold by the investor) would be exercised and other Put Option would expire unexercised. The net payoff would be the difference between the premiums of both the options **as reduced by** the difference between the exercise price of the Put Option sold and the price of the underlying.

The third possibility, that is to say, the price of the underlying being greater than the higher exercise price, happens, then both the options would expire unexercised, being out-of-money. In that case, our investor would end up earning the difference between the premium received on the written Put and the premium paid on the bought Put.

Explained in the next table is the conditional payoff flowing from the strategy just discussed.

Price of Stock	Payoff from Long Call	Payoff from Short Call	Total Payoff
$S_1 <= E_1$	$E_1 - S_1$	$S_1 - E_2$	$E_1 - E_2$
$E_1 < S_1 < E_2$	O (Not Exercised)	$S_1 - E_2$	$S_1 - E_2$
$S_1 >= E_2$	O (Not Exercised)	O (Not Exercised)	0

The same story is retold by this chart.

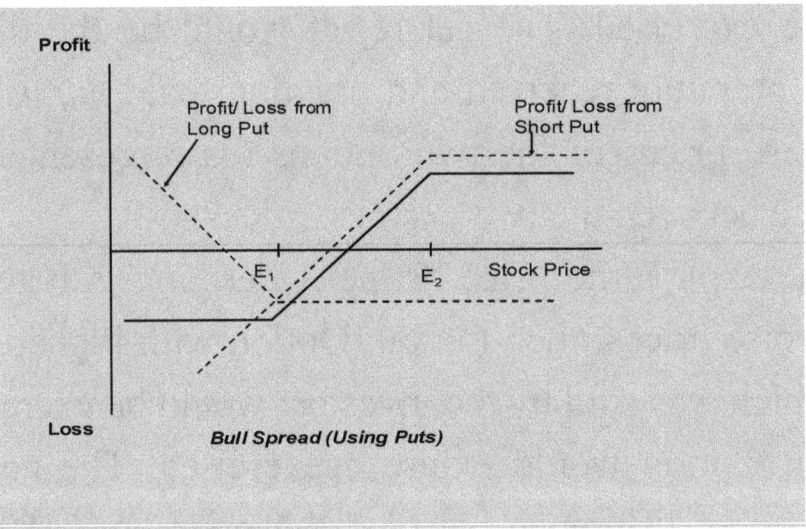

Bull Spread (Using Puts)

(7) Bear Spread Using Calls

This strategy is employed when the investor is bearish about the prices of the underlying. He, therefore, buys a Call Option on the underlying and writes a Call Option on the same underlying with the same maturity date, but with lower exercise price.

Here, also the premium difference between Call Option written and the Call Option bought would be the Net Inflow for the investor.

In case, the price of the underlying stock for which the Option contracts were entered, falls below the lower exercise price, then both the options would expire unexercised. So, the Net result would be the difference between the premium received and the premium paid on the respective options.

But, if turns out that the price of the underlying scrip is between the two exercise prices, then the Call Option with lower exercise price (which was sold) would be exercised and one with higher exercise price (which was bought) would not be exercised.

The result would be the loss as represented by the difference between the stock price and the lower exercise price (relating to the Call Option written and exercised). Of course, this loss would be reduced by the net inflow of premium received *minus* premium paid.

On the other hand, if the price of the underlying stock is higher than the higher exercise price, then both the Call Options would be exercised as they would both be in-the-money options under that situation. The loss to the investor would be the difference the exercise prices of the Call Options bought and sold.

Here, also this loss would be reduced by the net premium income arrived at by deducting premium paid on Call bought from the premium received on Call sold.

The tabular summary of this conditional payoff is given on the next page along with the pictorial presentation of the same.

Price of Stock	Payoff from Long Call	Payoff from Short Call	Total Payoff
$S_1 >= E_2$	$S_1 - E_2$	$E_1 - S_1$	$E_1 - E_2$
$E_1 < S_1 < E_2$	O (Not	$E_1 - S_1$	$E_1 - S_1$

	Exercised)		
$S_1 >= E_1$	O (Not Exercised)	O (Not Exercised)	0

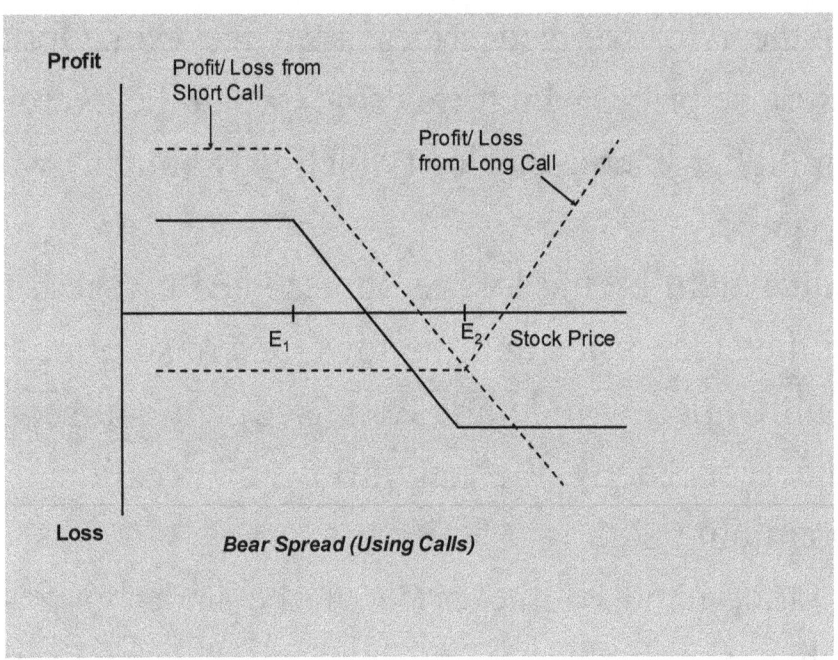

Bear Spread (Using Calls)

(8) Bear Spread Using Puts

Bear spreads, just like Bull spreads, can be created by using Put Options instead of Call Options. In such a case, the investor buys a Put Option with a high exercise price and sells one with a low exercise price. This would require an initial investment because the premium for put with a higher exercise price would be greater than the premium receivable for the put with lower exercise price, written by the investor.

The payoffs from a bear spread created with put options are given in the next table wherein the E_1 and E_2 are the exercise prices of the options sold and purchased respectively.

Price of Stock	Payoff from Long Call	Payoff from Short Call	Total Payoff

$S_1 >= E_2$	O (Not Exercised)	O (Not Exercised)	$E_1 - E_2$
$E_1 < S_1 < E_2$	$E_2 - S_1$	O (Not Exercised)	$E_2 - S_1$
$S_1 <= E_1$	$E_2 - S_1$	$S_1 - E_1$	0

Following is the graphical presentation of the above mentioned table

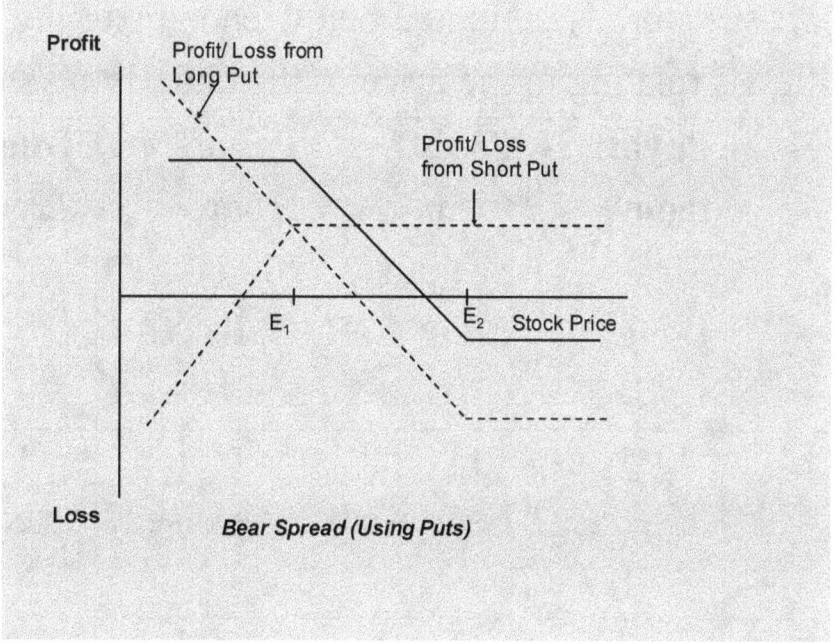

Bear Spread (Using Puts)

(9) Butterfly Spread

Butterfly spread results from taking positions in options with three different strike prices. In this strategy, the investor buys one Call Option with relatively low strike price E_1, also buys one Call Option with higher strike price E_3 along with writing *two* Call Options with the strike price E_2 which would be exactly half-way between the two strike prices E_1 and E_3.

The price E_2 would be usually close to the current market price of the underlying stock, with the result that a profit is pocketed if the stock price stays close to E_2 and a small loss would be incurred if there is a significant price movement either way from it. The strategy caters to the need of the investor who feels that huge price variations are not round the corner. However, positions taken entail some cost by way of premium on the options purchased.

The payoff structure is tabulated below encompassing various possibilities as relating to the price of the underlying stock.

Stock Price	Payoff from First Long Call (E_1)	Payoff form Second Long Call (E_3)	Payoff from Short Calls (E_2)	Total Payoff
$S_1 < E_1$	O (Not Exercised)	O (Not Exercised)	O (Not Exercised)	O (Not Exercised)
$E_1 <= S_1 < E_2$	$S_1 - E_1$	O (Not Exercised)	O (Not Exercised)	$S_1 - E_1$
$E_2 < S_1 < E_3$	$S_1 - E_1$	O (Not Exercised)	$2(E_2 - S_1)$	$E_3 - S_1$
$S_1 >= E_3$	$S_1 - E_1$	$S_1 - E_3$	$2(E_2 - S_1)$	0

The strategy can be more easily understood with the help of an example.

Suppose, RIL share is currently selling at Rs. 372. An investor, who feels that a significant change in this price is unlikely, in the next three months, observes the market prices of 3-month calls as tabulated on the next page:

Exercise Price (Rs.)	Call Price (Rs.)
365	11
370	8
375	6

The investor, here, decides to go long in two calls- one each with exercise price Rs. 365 and Rs. 375- and writes *two* calls with an exercise price of Rs. 370. So, his decision leads to **Butterfly Spread.** Buying two calls involves a payment of Rs. 11 + Rs. 6 = Rs. 17, and writing two calls yields Rs. 8 * 2 = Rs. 16. Thus, cost involved with the package of options = Rs. 17 – Rs. 16 = Re. 1.

Payoffs from this Butterfly Spread are given in the next following table:

Stock Price	Payoff from First Long Call (E_1 = 365)	Payoff form Second Long Call (E_3 = 375)	Payoff from Short Calls (E_2 = 370)	Total Payoff
$S_1 < 365$	O (Not Exercised)	O (Not Exercised)	O (Not Exercised)	O (Not Exercised)
$365 <= S_1 < 370$	$S_1 - 365$	O (Not Exercised)	O (Not Exercised)	$S_1 - 365$
$370 < S_1 <$	$S_1 - 365$	O (Not	$2(370 - S_1)$	$375 - S_1$

375		Exercised)		
$S_1 >= 375$	$S_1 - 365$	$S_1 - 375$	$2(370 - S_1)$	0

From the table, it is clear that when the price of an RIL share is less than Rs. 365 or greater than Rs. 375, the payoff will be nil, while if the price varied between Rs. 365 and Rs. 370, the payoff would be the price in excess of Rs. 365 and if it is in the range of Rs. 370 to Rs. 375, then the payoff is Rs. 375 **minus** the stock price.

The following table gives the calculation of Net result for four different given prices.

Price of RIL share	Total Payoff from Calls	Cost of Strategy	Net Result
63	0	(1)	(1)
68	3	(1)	2
73	2	(1)	1
80	0	(1)	(1)

Graphical presentation of the Butterfly strategy would be as under:

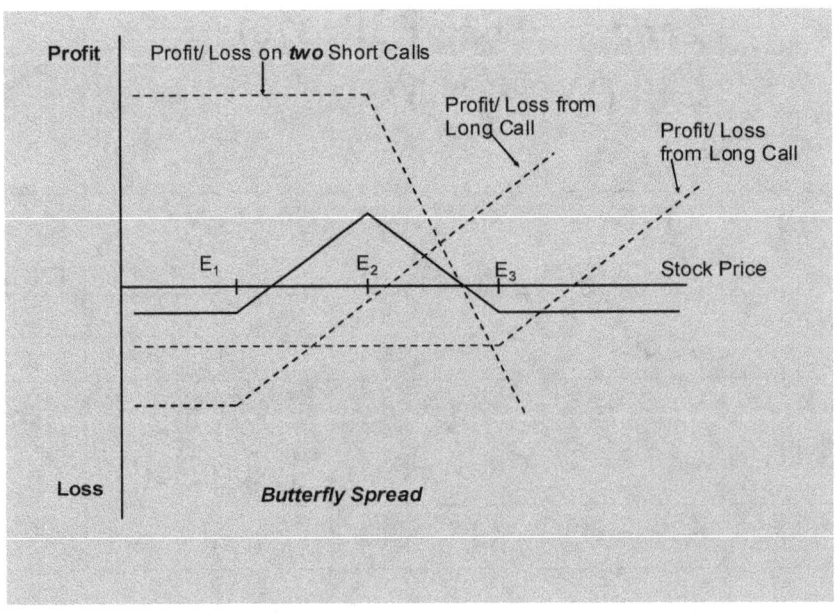

45

(10) Straddle

Straddle involves buying both the Call as well as the Put Option with the same exercise price and date of expiration. Since this strategy requires buying both the options, it costs to buy a straddle and to that extent, a loss is incurred if the price does not move away from the exercise price since in that case none of these options would be exercised. Buying a straddle is an appropriate strategy to adopt when large price changes are expected in the price of the underlying stock- for lower prices put will be exercised and for the higher prices, the call option will be exercised.

One practical example on the strategy would make things more clear.

Straddle, as has been mentioned just above, is undertaken when significant price movements are expected in the prices of the underlying. Generally, this happens when an outcome of an event, having a bearing on the fate of the company and in turn its stock prices, is uncertain. So, straddle is a cushion against an event risk, not only that, it also provides a great opportunity to make a profit should the prices move either way from the exercise price by a great many ticks.

For example, the market did not know the outcome of the Cabinet Committee on Disinvestment meeting when it was slated to be held on 7 September, 2002. The decision to delay disinvestment in HPCL and BPCL sent the stock prices plummeting.

With a great deal of certainty, one can say that a decision in favor of disinvestment would have sent the stock prices soaring. There was uncertainty in which direction the stock prices would have moved, prior to the event. The best strategy to beat this uncertainty would have been to buy a straddle.

The strategy would be beneficial if the increase or decrease is greater than the combined premium paid for Call as well as Put Options.

Suppose, if one bought BPCL Call and Put Options for a strike price of Rs. 240 by paying a premium of Rs. 10 and Rs. 5 respectively and based on the news of disinvestment delay, the prices fell to Rs. 210, one would have made a profit of Rs. 15. On the other hand, had the disinvestment measures been announced and the stock would have gone to Rs. 260, one would have made a profit of Rs. 5.

The chart showing the Net payoff as a function of the stock price of BPCL is shown below.

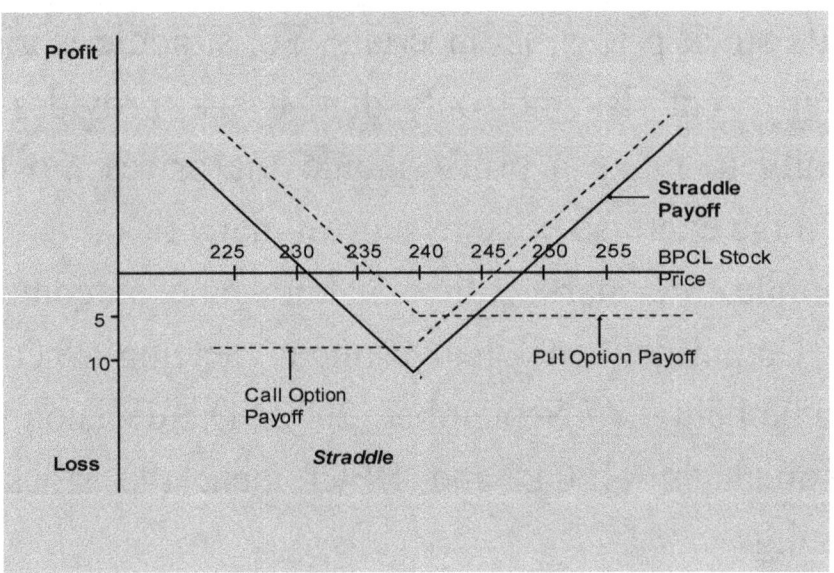

(11) Strip

Like straddles, strips and straps also involve taking long or short positions in calls and puts. **A strip** results when a long position in one call is coupled with a long position in two puts, all with the same exercise price and date of expiration. Here the investor is expecting that a big price movement in the stock price will take place but a decrease in the stock price is more likely than an increase.

Since a put option is profitable when a price decrease occurs, two puts are bought in this strategy. Accordingly, the profit function for the strategy, as shown in the following chart, is steeper in the lower than exercise price range and less steep in the region of higher prices.

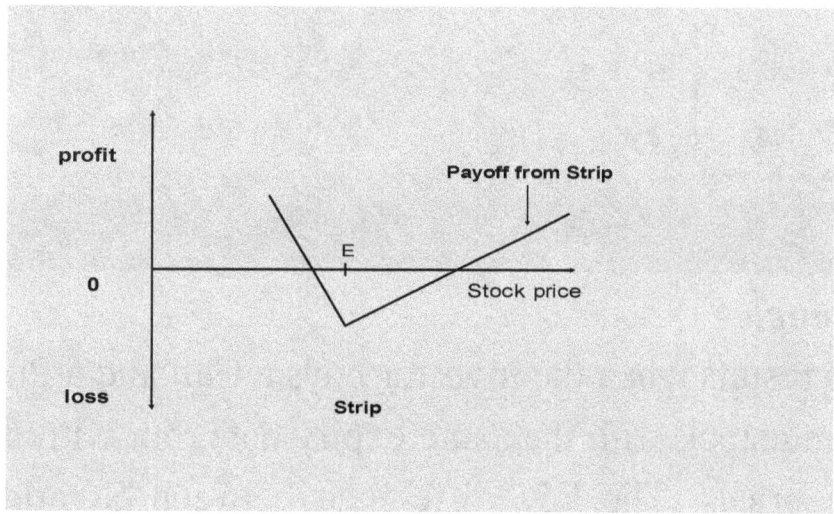

(12) Strap

Strap is employed when the investor expects that a big price change would occur, but the probability of the stock price going up is far higher than that of stock price going down. In such a situation buying a Put Option is matched with buying *two* Call Options.

As the investor's sentiment about the likely price of the scrip on the expiry day is bullish, he would prefer taking a long position in Call Options to that in the Put Option.

That is why he tends to buy *two* Call Options as against one Put Option, a tendency exactly opposite of one in **Strip** where he considered himself better off going long more in Put Options than in Call Options due to bearish sentiment then.

The payoff profile is shown in the following chart:

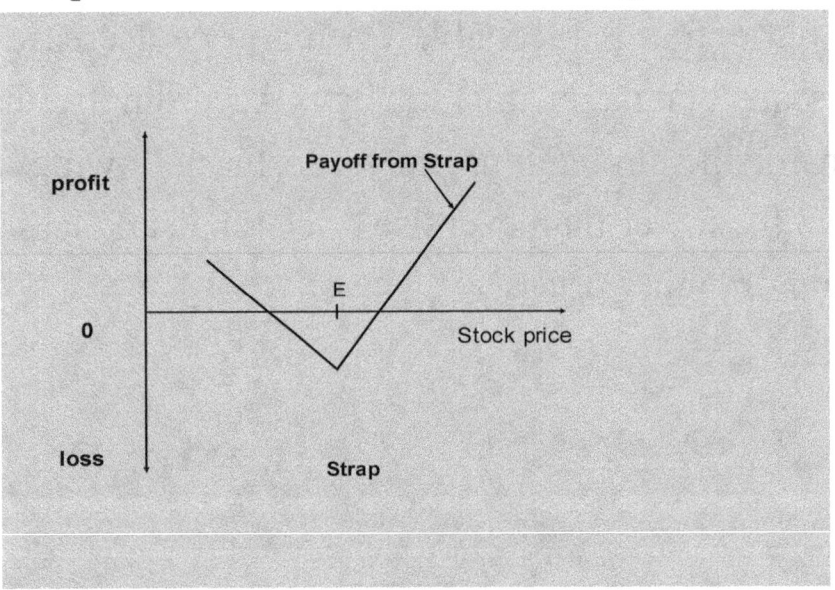

(13) Strangle

Strangle results when the investor buys a Call and a Put on the underlying stock with the same expiry date, but with different exercise prices. The key difference between **Straddle and Strangle** is that in case of the former, the exercise price of both the options (Call and Put) are same whereas in the latter's case, they are different.

The exercise price of the Put Option bought is lower than the exercise price of the Call Option bought. So, Strangle is a suitable strategy for the investor who believes that a sharp movement in the price of the stock is in the offing.

Suppose, E_1 is the exercise price of the Put Option and E_2 is the exercise price of the Call Option. The payoff table for this strangle is as follows:

Price of Stock	Payoff from Put	Payoff from Call	Total Payoff
$S_1 <= E_1$	$E_1 - S_1$	O (Not Exercised)	$E_1 - S_1$
$E_1 < S_1 < E_2$	O (Not Exercised)	O (Not Exercised)	O
$S_1 > E_2$	O (Not Exercised)	$S_1 - E_2$	$S_1 - E_2$

This payoff table is diagrammed in the chart on the next following page.

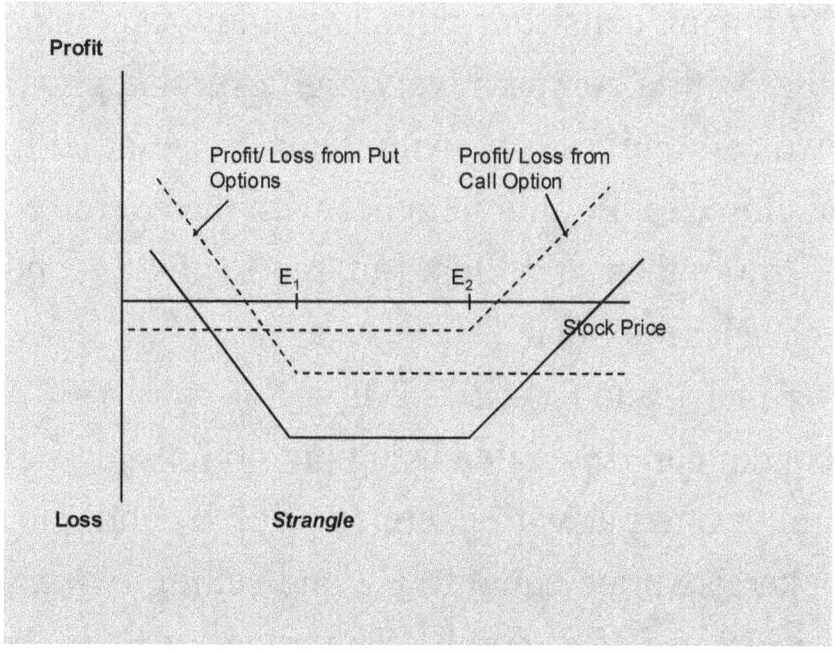

Evidently, a strangle is a strategy similar to straddle, as here as well, the investor is betting that a large price

change would take place but is not sure as to the direction in which the change would occur. However, in a strangle, the stock price has to move farther, than in a straddle, in order that the investor makes a profit. Also, if the stock price happens to be between the two exercise prices, the downside risk is smaller with a strangle than it is with a straddle if the price is close to exercise price.

This strangle is also termed as **bottom vertical combination** or **long strangle.** Similarly, a strangle may be sold. A **short strangle** is the choice of an investor who believes that large variations are unlikely. However, if they do occur, then larger amounts of losses are imminent.

(14) Long Condor

A condor, as an investment strategy, encompasses four call or four put options. A **long condor** involving call options is created by buying calls- one with a very low exercise price E_1 and another with a comparatively high exercise price E_4- and selling two call options- one with the exercise price E_2 higher than, and closer to, E_1 and the other with the exercise price E_3 which is lower than and closer to E_4. E_1, E_2, E_3 and E_4 are chosen in such a way that

$E_2 - E_1 = E_4 - E_3$, and $E_3 - E_1 = 2(E_2 - E_1)$

A long condor can be created using put options also. Here, the investor buys one put with exercise price E_1 and another one with an exercise price equal to E_4, and selling two puts- with the exercise prices of E_2 and E_3. The prices of E_1, E_2, E_3 and E_4 are related to each other as in the case of a long condor with call options.

Following is the picturesque presentation of the conditional payoff from the long condor using Call Options.

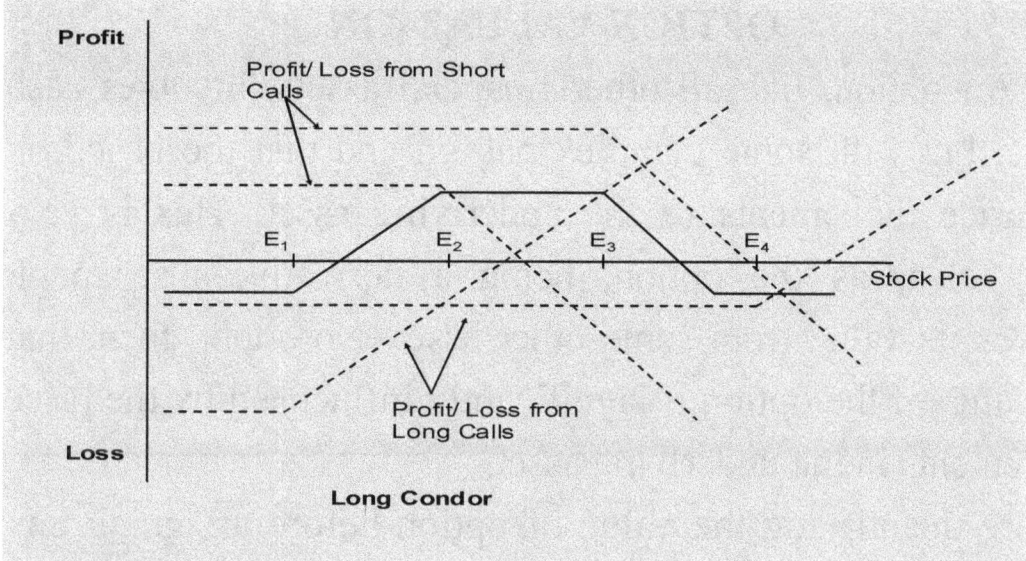

(15) Short Condor

A **short condor,** on the other hand, results by reversing the preceding strategy, and involving selling two calls having exercise prices of E_1 and E_4, and buying two calls with the exercise prices of E_2 and E_3.

As compared to Strangle, profit/ loss in case of Condors is limited in case large deviations from exercise prices are observed in stock prices on expiry.

The phenomenon of Short Condor is explained below through the help of the chart.

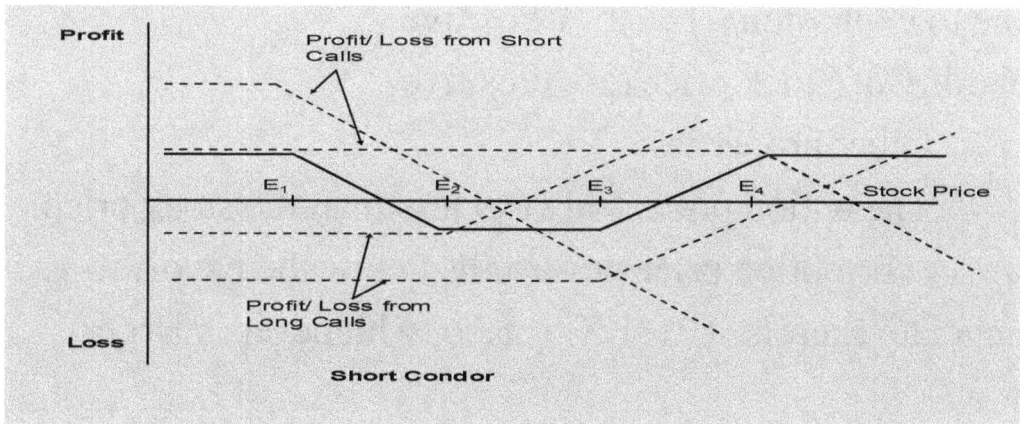

Chapter 8
Option Valuation
OPTION VALUATION

An option, like all other financial assets, involves cash flows, but with some complex pattern and that too based on the price movements of the underlying asset. This is very much clear as the option, being a derivative instrument, derives its value from some other asset. No doubt, then, that the value of the option is significantly influenced by the price movements in the underlying asset.

Before quantifying the value of option-before assigning any concrete Rupee tag to the option, let us first see some qualitative aspects or characteristics of the options value vis-à-vis changes in certain parameters.

What the price of a Call Option depends on?

1.   Increase in variables:

If there is an increase in: The change in the Call Option price is:

Stock Price (P)	Positive
Exercise Price (EX)	Negative
Interest Rate (r_f)	Positive[*]
Time to expiration (t)	Positive
Volatility of Stock price (	Positive[*]

2.   Other properties:

a.   The option price is always less than the stock price.

b.   The option price never falls below the payoff to immediate exercise (P – EX or zero, whichever is larger).

c.   If the stock is worthless, the option price approaches the stock.

d.   As the stock price becomes very large, the option price approaches the stock price less the present value of the exercise price.

[*] The direct effects of increases in r_f or $\square$ on option price are positive. There may also be indirect effects. For example, an increase in r_f could reduce stock price P. this in turn can reduce option price.

Given the complex and very much conditional payoff structure of options, it is very much difficult to value them. However, unlike other financial instruments, options cannot be valued using standard operating procedure of (1)forecasting expected cash flow and (2) discounting at the opportunity cost of capital. The first step is messy but feasible. Finding the opportunity cost of capital is impossible, because the risk of the option changes every time the stock price moves, and we know it will move along a random walk through the option's lifetime. It also changes over time even with the stock price constant.

When one buys a Call, he is actually taking a position in the stock but putting up less of his own money than if he had bought the stock directly. Thus, an option is always riskier than the underlying stock. It has a higher beta and a higher standard deviation of return.

How much riskier the option is depends on the stock price relative to the exercise price. An option that is in the money (stock price greater than exercise price in case of a Call) is safer than one that is out of money (stock price less than the exercise price in case of a Call).

Thus, a stock price increases raises the option's price and its risk increases. That is why the expected rate of return investor's demand from an option changes day by day, or hour by hour, every time the stock price moves.

Having seen the complexity involved in the valuation of options, now we come to know why an option-valuation technique eluded many economists for so many years.

However, an answer to this mystery came from two economists: Fisher Black and Myron Scholes. In their seminal contribution in the area of option valuation, they propounded a model to value the options, popularly known as "Black and Scholes Model".

This model was based on the earlier "Binomial Model" for option valuation. In fact, it would not be out of place to say that "Black and Scholes Model" was a refinement, or for that matter to say, an extension of "Binomial Model".

BLACK & SCHOLES MODEL FOR OPTION VALUATION

Noted economists Fisher Black and Myron Scholes, in their celebrated contribution in the area of option-valuation came out with the formula meant for the purpose. The formula for the model is somewhat unpleasant, yet it is the most reliable of all the models around. With some modifications, the model can also be used to value other financial options like currency options, interest rate options and so on.

According to the model, the value of a Call Option is calculated as follows:

$$C = S_0 N(d_1) - E e^{-rt} N(d_2)$$

Where,

$$d_1 = \frac{\ln(S_0/E) + (r + 0.5\sigma^2)t}{\sigma * sqrt(t)}$$

$$d_2 = \frac{\ln(S_0/E) + (r - 0.5\sigma^2)t}{\sigma * sqrt(t)}$$

C = current value of the option

r = continuously compounded risk-free rate of return

S_0 = current price of the stock

E = exercise price of the option

t = time remaining before the expiration date (expressed as a fraction of a year)

σ = Std. deviation of the continuously compounded annual rate of return

ln = natural logarithm

N(d) = value of the cumulative normal distribution evaluated at d.

Now, we see the assumptions underlying "Black and Scholes Model":

1. The option being valued is a European style option, with no possibility of an early exercise.

2. There are no transaction costs and there are no taxes.

3. The risk-free interest rate is known and constant over the life of the option.

4. The volatility of the underlying instrument (may be the equity share or the index) is known and constant over the life of the option.

5. The distribution of the possible share prices (or index levels) at the end of a period of time is log normal or, in other words, a share's continuously compounded rate of return follows a normal distribution. Essentially, this means that the share (or index) in question is ratio, with the added implication that the share prices (or indices) cannot become negative.

Now, we see one real life practical example of how Black and Scholes Model is used to find out the value of an option.

We have taken data of weekly closing prices of BPCL share for last 40 weeks starting from 7th June, 2002 to 13th March, 2003.

Table showing weekly closing prices of BPCL share at NSE and other relevant calculation

Date	Week	Closing Price of BPCL share (Rs.)	Price Relative	ln PR = X
7-Jun-02	1	251.3		
14-Jun-02	2	290.9	1.1576	0.1463
21-Jun-02	3	263.75	0.9067	-

				0.0980
28-Jun-02	4	267.3	1.0135	0.0134
5-Jul-02	5	284.65	1.0649	0.0629
12-Jul-02	6	288.55	1.0137	0.0136
19-Jul-02	7	300.15	1.0402	0.0394
26-Jul-02	8	302.4	1.0075	0.0075
2-Aug-02	9	291.35	0.9635	-0.0372
9-Aug-02	10	289.9	0.9950	-0.0050
16-Aug-02	11	287.75	0.9926	-0.0074
23-Aug-02	12	293.5	1.0200	0.0198
30-Aug-02	13	274.8	0.9363	-0.0658
6-Sep-02	14	253.5	0.9225	-0.0807
13-Sep-02	15	206.05	0.8128	-0.2072
20-Sep-02	16	193.8	0.9405	-0.0613
27-Sep-02	17	186.55	0.9626	-0.0381
4-Oct-02	18	182.1	0.9761	-0.0241
11-Oct-02	19	204.8	1.1247	0.1175
18-Oct-02	20	193.9	0.9468	-

				0.0547
25-Oct-02	21	189	0.9747	-0.0256
1-Nov-02	22	193.8	1.0254	0.0251
8-Nov-02	23	187.75	0.9688	-0.0317
15-Nov-02	24	185.65	0.9888	-0.0112
22-Nov-02	25	184.65	0.9946	-0.0054
29-Nov-02	26	190.65	1.0325	0.0320
6-Dec-02	27	216.55	1.1359	0.1274
13-Dec-02	28	219.2	1.0122	0.0122
20-Dec-02	29	210.65	0.9610	-0.0398
27-Dec-02	30	218.8	1.0387	0.0380
3-Jan-03	31	231	1.0558	0.0543
10-Jan-03	32	230.15	0.9963	-0.0037
17-Jan-03	33	227.9	0.9902	-0.0098
24-Jan-03	34	214.45	0.9410	-0.0608
31-Jan-03	35	192	0.8953	-0.1106
7-Feb-03	36	203.25	1.0586	0.0569
14-Feb-03	37	206.3	1.0150	0.0149

21-Feb-03	38	222.85	1.0802	0.0772
28-Feb-03	39	223.8	1.0043	0.0043
7-Mar-03	40	215.1	0.9611	-0.0396
13-Mar-03	41	209.15	0.9723	-0.0281

Price Relative means current week's closing price plus dividends, divided by previous week's closing price. For the sake of simplicity, here it has been assumed that no dividends have been paid out during the period covered.

Chapter 9
Puts Are Calls, Calls Are Puts

PUTS ARE CALLS, CALLS ARE PUTS

Bizarre as it might sound, the title is truer than anything else. Actually, this is what "Put Call Parity Theorem" says. As we know Puts and Calls represent basic options. They serve as building blocks for developing more complex options. "Put Call Parity Theorem" does just that.

The theorem involves a complex combination that consists of

(i)   buying a stock,

(ii)   buying a put option on that stock, and

(iii)   borrowing an amount equal to the exercise price.

The payoff from this combination is identical to the payoff from buying a call option. The algebra of this equivalence is shown as follows:

Constituents of the combination	Payoff before expiration if $S_1 < E$	Payoff before expiration if $S_1 >= E$
Buy the equity stock	S_1	S_1
Buy a put option	$E - S_1$	0
Borrow an amount equal to the exercise	$- E$	$- E$

price		
TOTAL	**0**	**$S_1 - E$**

The payoff from the individual components and the combination are shown in the following figure:

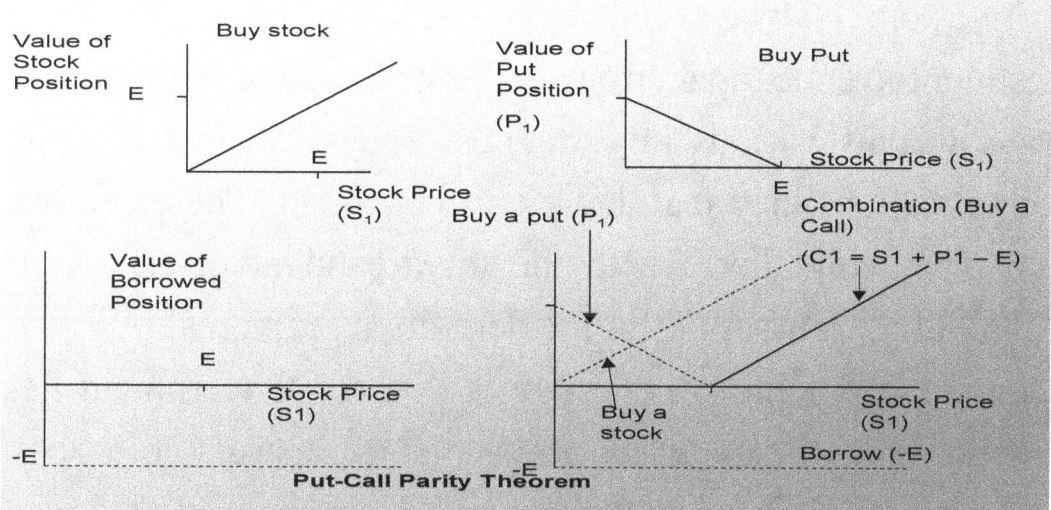

Put-Call Parity Theorem

If C_1 is the terminal value of the Call Option (for a call option, C_1 = Max (S_1–E, 0), P_1 the terminal value of the put option (for a put option, P_1 = Max (E–S_1, 0), S_1 the price of the stock, and E the amount borrowed, we know from the preceding analysis that:

$$C_1 = S_1 + P_1 - E$$

This is nothing but what "Put-Call Parity Theorem" seeks to explain.

Chapter 10
Taxability of Derivative Instruments

TAXABILITY OF DERIVATIVE INSTRUMENTS

An investor is always concerned with the taxability of an investment avenue, apart from the payoff arising out of it. He always weighs various investment avenues keeping in mind the implications they may have on his tax-bill. Therefore, we make an attempt here as to the tax treatment of the gains arising out of transactions in the derivative segments.

An interesting point to note here is that the Government has not come up with any direct provisions as regards the profits/ losses that result from the derivative instruments like Index Futures, Index Options, or for that matter, to say, any derivative instrument.

In the absence of any direct provision concerning this matter, we have to rely more on circulars or clarifications from CBDT. Though circulars can always be challenged in the court of law, for the time being, they provide invaluable insight into the subject-matter at hand.

While dealing with the taxability of such derivative transactions where settlement is done through Cash instead of actual delivery of ownership of the underlying asset, first section that comes into the picture is Section 73.

For the perusal of the reader, we have given under the verbatim of Section 73 of the Income Tax Act, 1961.

SECTION 73 Losses in speculation business

1.   Any loss, computed in respect of a speculation business carried on by the assessee, shall not be set off except against profits and gains, if any, of another speculation business.

2.   Where for any assessment year any loss computed in respect of a speculation business has not been wholly set off under sub-section (1), so much of the loss as is not so set off or the whole loss where the assessee had no income from any other speculation business, shall, subject to the other provisions of this chapter, be carried forward to the following assessment year,

And:

i.   It shall be set off against the profit and gains, if any, of any speculation business carried forward to the following assessment year; and

ii.   If the loss cannot be wholly set off, the amount of the loss not so set off shall be carried forward to the following assessment year and so on.

3.   In respect of allowance on account of depreciation or capital expenditure on scientific research, the provisions of sub-section (2) of section 72 shall apply in relation to speculation business as they apply in relation to any other business.

4.   No loss shall be carried forward under this section for more than eight assessment years immediately succeeding the assessment year for which the loss was first computed.

Explanation. – Where any part of the business of a company (other than a company whose gross total income

consists mainly of income which is chargeable under the heads "Interest on securities", "Income from house property", "Capital gains" and "Income from other sources" or a company the principal business of which is the business of banking or the granting of loans and advances) consists in the purchase and sale of shares of other companies, such company shall, for the purposes of this section, be deemed to be carrying on a speculation business to the extent to which the business consists of the purchase and sale of such shares.

The crux of this section is that losses arising out of speculation can be set off against the profits, if any, of the other speculation business of the assesssee. However, if, in the instant year, the assessee does not have sufficient profits from other speculation business, he can carry forward the said losses to the next years to be set off against the profits of the speculation business subject, of course, to the maximum of eight years.

Given this limited framework incorporated in the Act, we have to see what, according to the Act or CBDT, amounts to a speculative transaction.

Section 43(5) defines speculative transactions as those which are periodically or ultimately settled otherwise than by actual delivery or transfer. By this definition, all index futures transactions will qualify prima facie as speculative transactions, as delivery of such futures is not possible.

Exceptions are provided to this definition to cover cases where contracts are entered into in respect of stocks and shares by a dealer or investor to guard against losses in holdings of stocks and shares through price fluctuations.

Another exception is provided for contracts entered into by a member of a forward market or a stock exchange in the course of any transaction in the nature of jobbing or arbitrage to guard against losses, which may arise in the ordinary course of his business as such member.

The CBDT has issued a Circular No 23 dated 12th September 1960 on this area. The important provisions of this Circular are summarized below:

• Hedging sales can be taken to be genuine only to the extent the total of such transactions does not exceed the ready stock. Hedging transactions in connected, though not the same, commodities should not be treated as speculative transactions.

• It cannot be accepted that a dealer or investor in stocks or shares can enter into hedging transactions outside his holdings. By this interpretation, transactions in index futures will not be covered under the definition of 'hedging'.

• Speculation loss, if any carried forward from earlier years, should first be adjusted against speculation profits of the particular year before allowing any other loss to be adjusted against those profits.

The Explanation to Section 73 provides for the additional ground for the deemed speculation. It provides that where any part of the business of a company consists in the purchase and sale of shares of other companies, such company shall, for the purposes of this Section, be deemed to be carrying on a speculation business to the extent to which the business consists of purchase and sale of such shares. However, the said explanation has kept the following out of the ambit of the deemed speculation:

• Company whose Gross Total Income consists mainly of Income chargeable under the heads Interest on Securities, Income from House Property, Capital Gains and Income from Other Sources

• Company whose principal business is Banking and

• Company whose principal business is granting of loans and advances.

So, most brokers and dealers are currently caught within the mischief of this Explanation, especially after the wave of corporatization of brokers' businesses.

The Explanation, however, does not cover index futures.

In the light of the above-mentioned status quo, it is highly possible that the Income-Tax Department can take a stand whereby the index futures are considered as Speculation business and taxed accordingly.

Another possible view (as far as non-business assessees are concerned) could be that gains and losses from index futures be treated as short term capital gains. This view can gain support from the fact that such assessees are not covered within the ambit of Sections 43 and 73 referred to above.

However, the assessee can refute the said contention of the Department unless and until there is no direct provision that deem the index futures as a speculation transaction. The grounds of denial can be:

1.   Section 43(5) speaks of purchase and sale of any 'commodity', including shares and stocks. Index futures are not 'commodities'. Further, index futures are also not 'stocks and shares'. Hence, section 43(5) does not apply to futures transactions. The question of examining the provisos (exceptions) does not arise.

2.   Exceptions to 'speculative transactions' as provided in Section 43(5) also include hedging transactions undertaken in respect of stocks and shares. Proviso (b) to Section 43(5) states – 'a contract in respect of stocks and shares entered into by a dealer or investor therein to guard against loss in his holdings of stocks and shares through price fluctuations'. It however remains to be seen whether index futures can be covered under 'stocks and shares'. We hold the contention that if index futures are considered to be part of stocks and shares as per the wording of Section 43(5), then the proviso will also become applicable and hence hedging contracts through the mechanism of index futures will not be considered speculative. On the other hand, if index futures are not part of stocks and shares, then neither Section 43(5) nor the proviso apply and hence the entire gamut of index futures transactions will remain out of the purview of speculative transactions.

3.   Explanation to Section 73 speaks of purchase and sale of shares of other companies. Index futures are not 'shares'. Hence, this Explanation does not apply to futures transactions. It is believed and understood that foreign exchange forward transactions are currently not being caught within the mischief

of Sections 43 and 73. This lends more comfort to the possibility of index futures also being left out of this net, though only experience will indicate the stand the Income tax department will take as the Income-Tax Department is like a wife- you never know which way it will turn!

Section-II
Interest Rate And Other Derivative
Chapter 1
Forward Rate Agreements
FORWARD RATE AGREEMENTS

A Forward Rate Agreement (FRA) is notionally an agreement between two parties in which one of them (the seller of the FRA), contracts to lend to the other (the buyer), a specified amount of funds, in a specific currency, for a specified period starting at a specified future date, at an interest rate fixed at the time of agreement.

It is "notional" because in practice, actual lending or borrowing of the underlying principal does not take place but only the interest rate is locked in. the buyer of the FRA in turn agrees to borrow (again notionally), funds for a specified duration, starting at a specified future date, at a rate fixed at the time the FRA is bought.

A typical FRA quote from a bank might look like this:

USD 6/9 months: 7.50–7.60 % p.a.

This quote can be interpreted as follows:

❖ The bank is ready to accept a US dollar deposit at a date six months far from now for a period of three months, maturing nine months from now, at an interest rate of 7.50%p.a. This is called **bid rate.**

❖ The bank is also offering a three-month loan after six months from now at a rate of 7.60%p.a. This is termed as **ask rate.**

The following figure gives out the schematic presentation of an FRA, contracted at $t = 0$, applicable for the period between $t = S$ and $t = L$. DS and DL are actual number of days from $t = 0$ to $t = S$ and from $t = 0$ to $t = L$ respectively. The period from $t = S$ to $t = L$ is the contract period, $t = S$ is the settlement date, and DF is the number of days in the contract period.

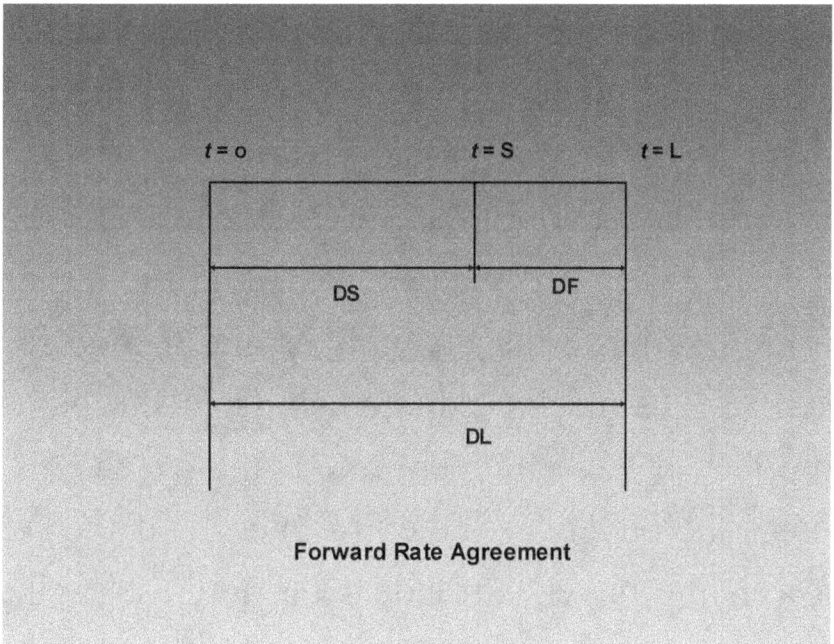

Forward Rate Agreement

The important point to note is that there is no exchange of principal amount. If the settlement rate on the settlement date is above the contract rate, the seller compensates the buyer for the difference in interest on the agreed upon principal amount for the duration of the period in the contract.

Conversely, if the settlement rate is below the contract rate, the buyer compensates the seller.

The compensation is paid up front on the settlement day and therefore has to be suitably discounted since interest payment on short-term loans is at maturity of the loan.

One of the following two formulas is used for calculating settlement payment from the seller to the buyer:

$$P = [(L-R) * DF * A] / [(B * 100) + (DF * L)]$$
$$P = [(R-L) * DF * A] / [(B * 100) + (DF * L)]$$

Here the notation is

L	=	The settlement rate (%)
R	=	The contract rate (%)
DF	=	The number of days in a contract period
A	=	The notional principal
B	=	Day count basis (360 or 365)

The first formula is used when L > R, and the payment P is from the FRA seller to the FRA buyer, the second formula is used when L < R and the payment is from the buyer to the seller. In effect, if the settlement rate is higher, the FRA seller compensates the buyer for the extra interest; if the settlement rate is lower, the buyer surrenders the interest saving to the seller.

An example along this line would render more clarity on the concept.

Suppose a bank quote for an FRA is as below:

USD 6/9 months: 7.20–7.30% p.a.

A company which intends to take a loan for a period of 3 months starting from the end of the sixth months from now wishes to lock in its borrowing rate. It buys the FRA from the bank which is giving the above FRA quotes, at the bank's ask rate of 7.30% for an underlying notional principal of USD 5 million. Suppose on settlement date, the reference rate, for instance, 3-month USD LIBOR is pegged at 8.5%. The number of days in the contract period is 91 and the basis is 360 days. The bank will have to pay the company

$= USD [(8.50-7.30)(91)(50,00,000)]/[(36000)+(91*8.50)]$

$= USD\ 14847.65$

FRAs are traded in all convertible currencies. The minimum principal amount is around 5 million units of a currency. Like the forward exchange contract, FRAs are an over-the-counter product and therefore not standardized.

Chapter 2
Swaps

SWAPS

In all the history of financial markets, no markets have ever grown or evolved as rapidly as have the swap markets.

This is a testament to the efficacy and flexibility of the instruments, the resourcefulness and the professionalism of the new breed of financial engineers, and the increased appreciation by financial managers of the importance of financial risk management in a volatile interest rate, exchange rate, and commodity price environment.

Industrial corporations, financial corporations, thrifts, banks, insurance companies, world organizations, and sovereign governments now use swaps.

Swaps are used to reduce the cost of capital, manage risks, exploit economies of scale, arbitrage the world's capital markets, enter new markets, and create synthetic instruments. A new user, new uses, and new swap variants emerge almost daily.

Most people with some exposure to swaps believe that swaps are exceedingly complex instruments. In reality, this seeming complexity is more in the extensive documentation needed to fully specify the contract terms and the myriad of specialty provisions that can be included to tailor the swap to some specific need.

This chapter demystifies basic or "plain vanilla" swap in the form of cash flow diagrams. By visually depicting the pattern of cash flows associated with swaps and the ways that swaps meld with cash market transactions, one can easily see how a desired end result is achieved.

The applicability of basic swaps are with respect to the following three different settings:

(1)   an interest rate swap to convert a fixed-rate obligation to a floating-rate obligations;

(2)   a currency swap to convert an obligation in one currency to an obligation in another currency; and

(3) A commodity swap to convert a floating prices to a fixed price.

Before presenting the swap model, however, a brief history of the swap product will put the instruments in perspective.

History of the Swap Product

The first currency swap was engineered in London in 1979. During the two years that followed the market remained small and obscure. This obscurity ended when, in 1981, Salomon Brothers put together what is now the landmark currency swap involving the World Bank and IBM. The stature of the parties gave long-term credibility to currency swaps.

It was a short step from currency swaps to interest rate swaps. Like the currency swap, the first interest rate swap was engineered in London. This took place in 1981.

The product was introduced to the United States the following year when the Student Loan Marketing Association (Salllie Mae) employed a fixed-for-floating interest rate swap to convert the interest-rate character of some of its liabilities.

Once established, the market for currency and interest rate swaps grew rapidly. From under $5 billion in combined notional principal outstandings at the end of 1982, the market grew to over $2.5 trillion by the end of 1990.

The financial institutions that originated the swap product first saw themselves in the role of brokers. That is, they would find the potential counterparties with matched needs and, for a commission, would assist the parties in the negotiation of a swap agreement.

The brokering of swaps proved more difficult than originally envisioned because of the need to precisely match each individual contract provision. It wasn't long, however, before these institutions realized their portnetial as dealers.

That is, they could make a more liquid market by playing the role of Counterparty. This was possible because of the existence of a large cash market for U.S. Treasury debt and well-developed futures markets in which the swap dealers could hedge their resultant exposures.

By 1984, representatives from leading dealer banks (commercial banks and investment banks) began work on standardizing swap documentations. In 1985 this group organized itself into the International Swap Dealers Association (ISDA) and published the first standardized swap code.

The code was revised in 1986. In 1987, the standardization efforts of the ISDA culminated in the publication of standard form agreements. These contracts are structured as master agreements.

As such, all subsequent swaps entered by the same counterparties are treated as supplements to the original agreement. Standardization of documentation dramatically reduced both the time and the cost of originating a swap.

Commodity swaps were the first engineered in 1986 by the Chase Manhattan Bank. But, no sooner was the mechanism for commodity swaps in place than the Commodity Futures Trading Commission (CFTC) cast a cloud over the product by questioning the legality of the contracts. The intervention of the CFTC brought that agency into direct conflict with ISDA and a lengthy battle ensued. At the same time, those banks involved in commodity swaps moved the bulk of their activity overseas.

In July of 1989, the CFTC issued a favorable policy statement on commodity swaps. The agency decided to grant the contracts a "safe harbor", provided that certain criteria were met.

These criteria were of little consequence as, for the most part, they reflected current industry practice. By the end of 1989 the volume of commodity swap outstandings was nearly $8 billion.

While still small in comparison to interest rate and currency swaps, there appears to be tremendous potential for this market.

Chapter 3
The Structure of A Swap

THE STRUCTURE OF A SWAP

A Note on Rate Conventions

Interest rate and currency swaps are often discussed together- in which case they are collectively called rate swaps. Since the inception of rate swaps, the floating-rate side has most often been tied to the London Interbank Offered Rate known by the acronym LIBOR. LIBOR is the rate of interest charged on interbank loans of Eurocurrency deposits.

While it is rarely made explicit, LIBOR is understood to be a quote on dollar deposits (Eurodollars). But non dollar LIBORs are also quoted. Deutschemark LIBOR, for example, would be denoted DEM LIBOR. All references to LIBOR in this chapter are references to dollar LIBOR unless specifically indicated otherwise.

LIBOR quotes are available for various terms including one-month deposits (1-M LIBOR), three-month deposits (3-M LIBOR), six-month deposits (6-M LIBOR), and one year deposits (1-Y LIBOR). Regardless of the length of the deposit, LIBOR, like all interest rates, is quoted on an annual basis. There are two complications, however, which we need to point out.

To determine the **effective annual rate** corresponding to a given term deposit, we need to take into considerations the number of days in a six-month period and the number of compounding per year. LIBOR, by convention, is quoted "actual over 360".

That is, the interest rate is stated as though the year has 360 days, but interest is actually paid every day. The effect of this is to raise the effective rate of interest. For example, if 6-M LIBOR is quoted at 8.00 percent, we would expect that the six-month periodic rate is 4 percent.

But, in fact, one would earn 182/360 * 8.00 percent rather than 0.5*8.00 percent. Thus, the periodic rate is 4.0444 percent. During the second half of the year, one would earn a periodic rate of 183/360*8.00 percent for a periodic rate of 4.0667 percent.

The second complication stems from the fact that the interest earned during the first half of the year would itself earn interest during the second half of the year. That is, compounding raises the effective annual rate of interest. To get the effective annual rate, we must take the compounding into account. This is done below:

$$ER=[(1.040444)*(1.040667)] - 1$$
$$= 8.276 \text{ percent}$$

We see then that the effective annual rate corresponding to a 6-M LIBOR quote of 8 percent is about 8.276 percent.

The reason that this is important is that the fixed-rate side of a rate swap, called the swap coupon, is most often quoted as bond equivalent (BEY) (also called a coupon equivalent yield). Bond equivalency yields are calculated on the basis of a 365-day year with quotes stated actual over 365.

This differing treatment implies that LIBOR rate differentials and swap coupon differentials are not directly comparable. In order to properly compare them, they must first be adjusted for the differing numbers of days on which the two rates are quoted.

Most often, this adjustment takes the form of a simple multiplication of a rate differential 365/360 (when going from LIBOR to BEY) or 360/365 (when going from BEY to LIBOR).

This adjustment is only correct, however, if the payment frequencies on the two sides (legs) of the swap are the same- i.e. They are both made quarterly, or both made semiannually or both made annually.

The floating-rate side of a swap need not be tied to LIBOR. It can be tied to some other readily identifiable rate that is not easily manipulated by an interested party. The rate can and often is tied to a rate index or based on an average of observations on a short-term rate or a rate index.

Frequently used rates include certificate of deposit, commercial paper, T-bill, Fed funds, and the Twelfth District cost of funds. Nevertheless, the floating-rate side of most rate swaps are LIBOR based.

The Basic Structure of a Swap

All swaps are built around the same basic structure. Two parties, called counterparties, agree to one or more exchanges of specified quantities of underlying assets.

We call the quantities of underlying assets in a swap the notionals in order to distinguish them from physical exchanges in the cash markets, which are called actuals.

A swap may involve one exchange of notionals, two exchanges of notionals, a series of exchanges of notionals, or no exchanges of notionals.

Most often, a swap involves one exchange of notionals at the commencement of the swap and a reexchange upon the swap's termination.

The notionals exchanged in a swap may be the same or different. Between the exchanges of notionals, the counterparties make payments to each other for the use of the underlying assets.

The first Counterparty makes periodic payments at a fixed price for the use of the second counterparty's assets. This fixed price is called the swap coupon. At the same time, the second counterparty makes the periodic payments at a floating (market determined) price for the use of the first counterparty's assets.

This is the basic or "plain vanilla" structure. By modifying the terms appropriately and/or adding specialty provisions, this simple structure can be converted to dozens of variants to suit specific end user needs.

For purposes of illustrations, we shall call the first counterparty A and the second counterparty B.

It is very difficult to arrange a swap directly between two end users. A much more efficient structure is to involve a financial intermediary that serves as counterparty to both end users. This Counterparty is called a swap dealer, a market maker, or a swap bank. The terms are used interchangeably. The swap dealer profits from the bid-ask spread it imposes on the swap coupon.

The cash flows associated with a typical swap are illustrated in the following figures:

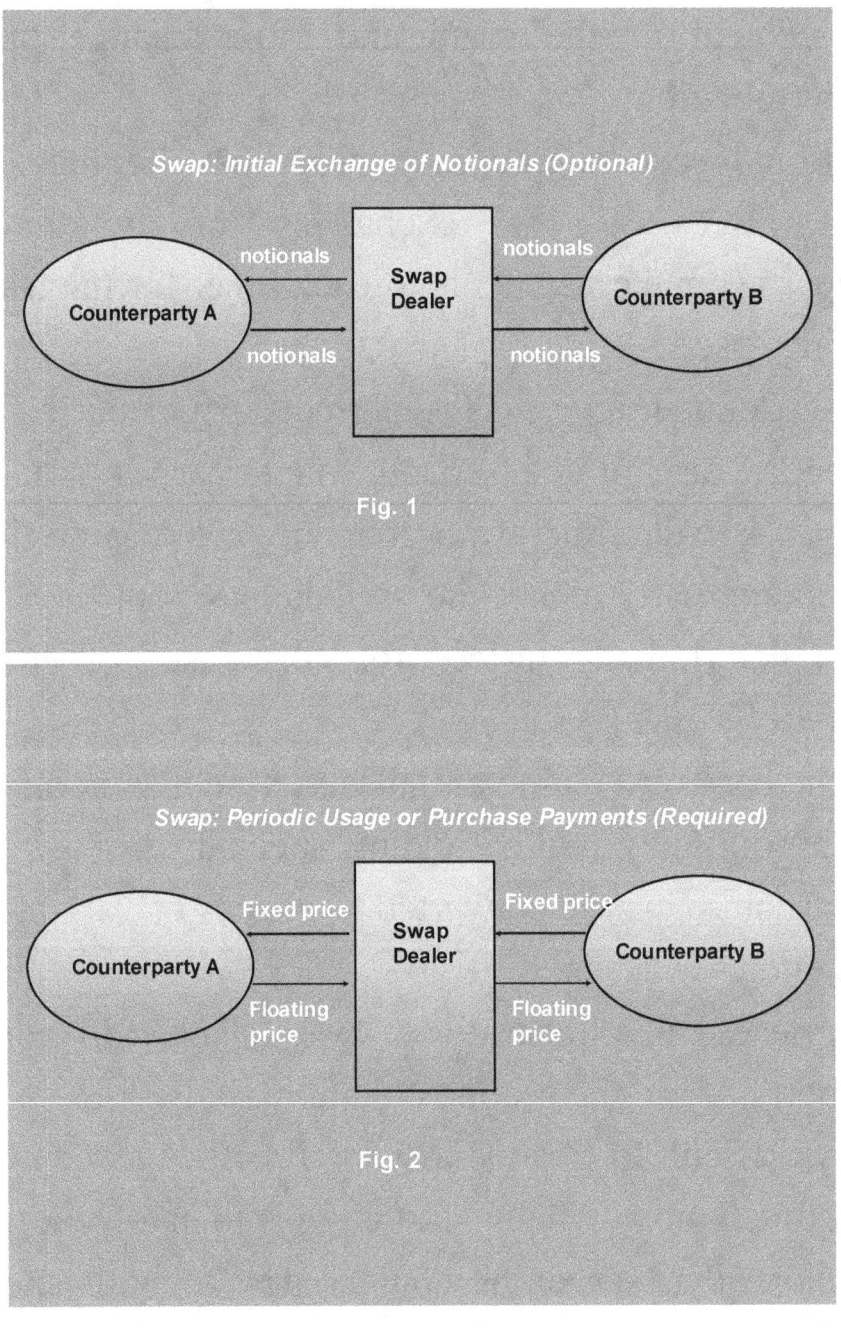

Fig. 1

Fig. 2

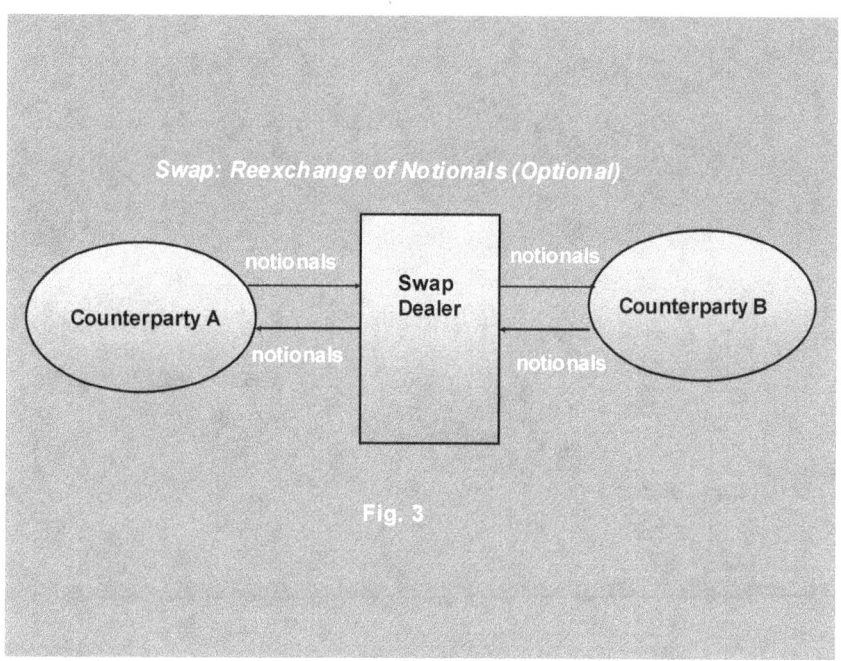

Swap: Reexchange of Notionals (Optional)

Fig. 3

The first figure depicts the initial exchange of notionals, which is optional in the sense that it is not required in all swaps; the second figure depicts the periodic usage payments; and the third figure depicts the reexchange of notionals, which, like the initial exchange of notions, is optional in the sense that it is not required in all swaps.

A swap by itself would generally not make much sense. But swaps do not exist in isolation. They are used in conjunction with appropriate cash market positions or transactions. There are three basic transactions:

(1)   Obtain "actuals" from the cash market,

(2)   make (receive) payments to (from) the cash market, or

(3)   supply actuals to the cash market. These possibilities are summarized in the next figure. The cash markets depicted in the figure may be the same or different.

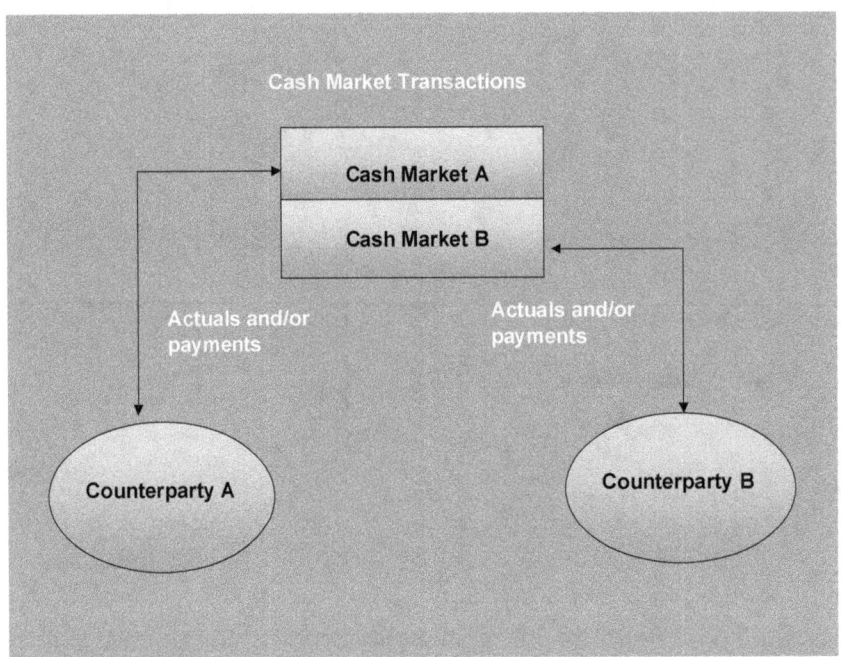

By combining the cash market transactions with an appropriately structured swap, we can engineer a great many different outcomes. The idea of interest rate swaps and currency swaps developed in the later chapters.

Chapter 4
Interest Rate Swaps
INTERST RATE SWAPS

In **Interest-Rate Swaps**, the exchangeable notionals take the form of quantities of money and are consequently called **notional principals**. In such a swap, the notional principals to be exchanged are identical in amount and involve the same currency.

As such, they can be dispensed with-, which explains the origin of the term **notional**. Furthermore, since the periodic usage payments, called interest in this case, are also in the same currency, only the value differential needs to be exchanged on the periodic settlement dates.

Interest rate swaps are often motivated by a desire to reduce the cost of financing. In these cases, one party has access to comparatively cheap fixed-rate funding, but desires floating-rate funding while another party has access to comparatively cheap floating-rate funding but desires fixed-rate funding.

By entering into swaps with a swap dealer, both parties can obtain the form of financing they desire and simultaneously exploit their comparative borrowing advantages.

For example, suppose that Party A is in need of 10-year debt financing. Party A has access to comparatively cheap floating-rate financing but desires a fixed-rate obligation.

For purposes of illustration, assume that Party A can borrow at a floating rate of LIBOR + 50 bps or at a semiannual (sa) fixed rate of 11.25 percent. As it happens, Party B is also in need of 10-year debt financing. Party B has access to comparatively cheap fixed-rate rate financing but desires a floating-rate obligation. For the purpose of illustration, assume that Party B can borrow fixed rate at a semiannual rate of 10.25 percent and can borrow floating rate as sixth-month LIBOR.

As it happens, Party A desires fixed-rate funding and Party B desires floating-rate funding.

The swap dealer stands ready to enter a swap as either fixed-rate payer (floating-rate receiver) or as floating-rate payer (fixed-rate receiver). In both cases, the dealer's floating rate is six-month LIBOR.

Under its present pricing, if the dealer is to be the fixed-rate payer, it will pay a swap coupon of 10.40 percent (sa). If the dealer is to be fixed-rate receiver, it requires a swap coupon of 10.50 percent (sa).

The financial engineers working for a swap dealer suggest that Party A issue floating-rate debt and that Party B issue fixed-rate debt and that they both enter into swaps with the swap dealer. Party A, now called Counterparty A, enters a swap, with the swap dealer acting as a floating-rate payer; and Party B, now called Counterparty B, enters a swap, with the dealer acting as a fixed-rate payer. While there are no exchanges of notional principals in these swaps, there are still three types of exchanges if we include the borrowings in the cash market.

The full set of cash flows is illustrated in the following figures:

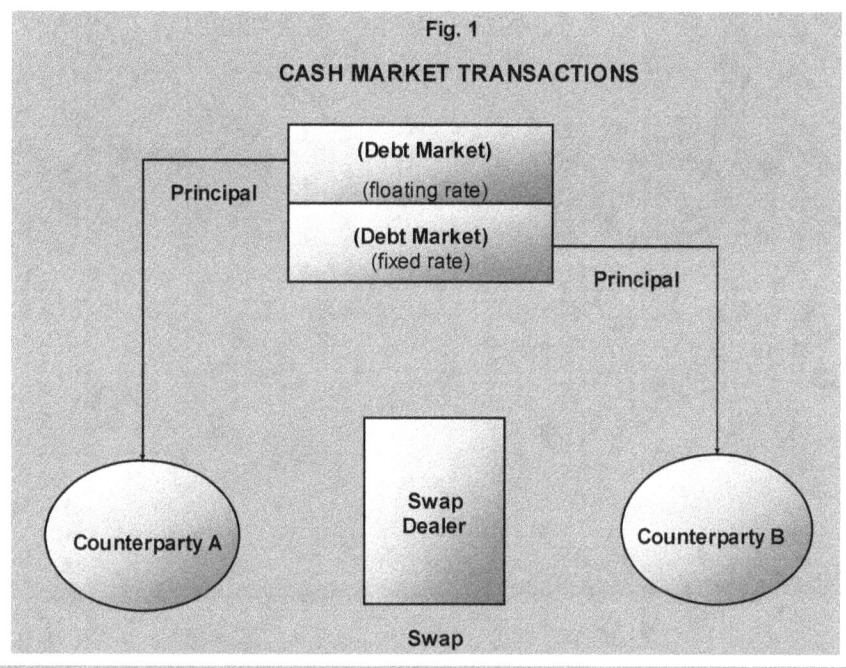

Fig. 1
CASH MARKET TRANSACTIONS

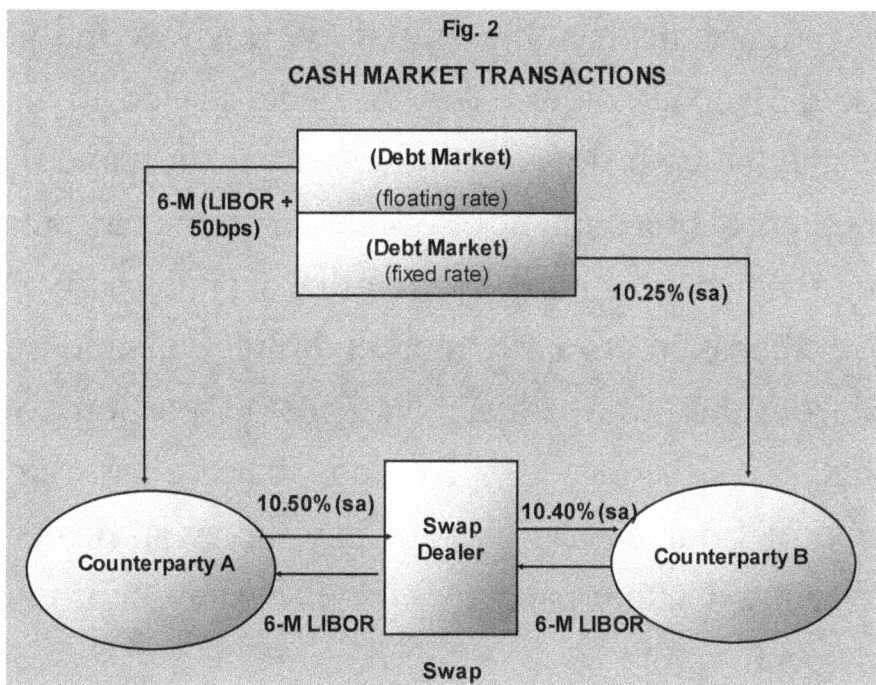

Fig. 2
CASH MARKET TRANSACTIONS

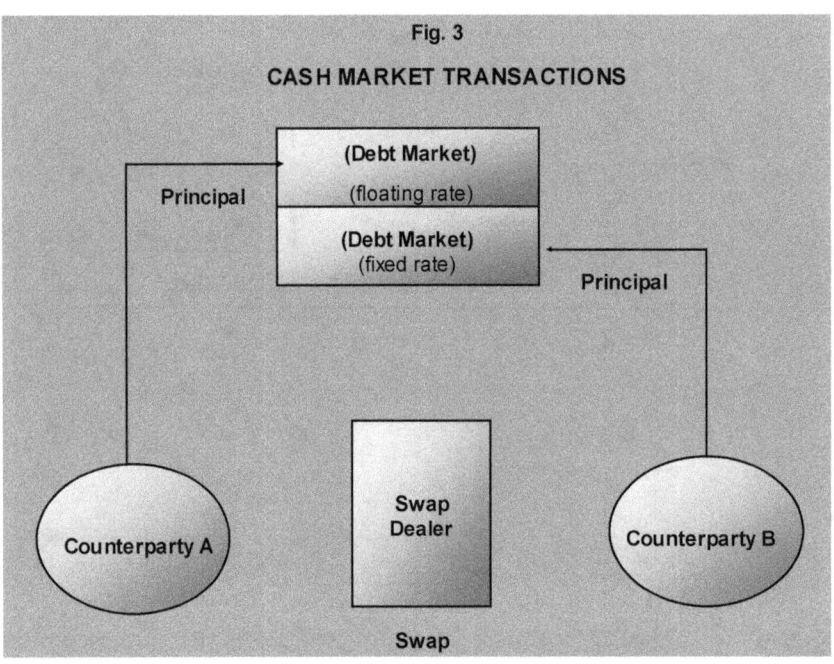

Fig. 3

CASH MARKET TRANSACTIONS

The first figure depicts the initial borrowings in the cash markets; the second figure depicts debt service in the cash markets and the cash flows with the swap dealer; and the third figure depicts the repayment of principals in the cash market.

Examine the second figure. Notice that Counterparty A pays LIBOR+ 50bps on its cash market obligation and receives LIBOR from the swap dealer. The LIBOR portions of these payments are, therefore, offsetting. The only remaining obligation of Counterparty A is to pay the swap dealer 10.50 percent. Thus, Counterparty A's final cost is approximately 11.00 percent.

This is an approximation because, as noted earlier, the 50 basis point differential is not directly comparable to the foxed rate. It must first be adjusted by multiplying by 365/360.

After this adjustment, we see that the real cost to Counterparty A is closer to 11.01 percent. Since direct borrowing of fixed rate in the cash market would have cost Counterparty A 11.25

percent, it is clear that Counterparty A has been benefited by 24 bps by employing the swap.

Counterparty B is paying a fixed rate of 10.25 percent on its cash market borrowing and receiving 10.40 percent from the swap dealer. Thus, the total cost of Counterparty B is ahead by 15 basis points. In addition, Counterparty B is paying the swap dealer LIBOR.

Thus, the total cost of Counterparty B's debt is approximately LIBOR- 15 bps (even after adjusting the differential by 360/365). Had Counterparty B borrowed floating rate directly, it would have paid LIBOR. Thus, we find that the swap has saved Counterparty B 15 bps.

As a side point, notice that the swap dealer earns 10 bps for its services in making a liquid swap market. This 10bps is the difference between the swap coupon received from Counterparty A and the swap coupon paid to Counterparty B.

Chapter 5
Currency Swap
CURRENCY SWAPS

In a **Currency Swap**, the currencies in which the principals are denominated are different, and for this reason, usually (but not always) need to be exchanged. A currency swap is viable whenever one counterparty has comparatively cheaper access to one currency than it does to another.

To illustrate, suppose that Counterparty A can borrow deutschemark for seven years at a fixed rate of 9.0 percent and can borrow seven-year dollars at a floating-rate of one-year LIBOR. Counterparty B, on the other hand, can borrow seven-year deutschemark at a rate of 10.1 percent and can borrow seven-year floating-rate dollars at a rate of one-year LIBOR.

As it happens, Counterparty A needs floating-rate dollar financing and Counterparty B needs fixed-rate deutschemark financing.

The financial engineers working for a swap dealer that makes deutschemark-for-dollar currency swaps work out a solution. The dealer is currently prepared to pay a fixed rate of 9.45 percent on deutschemark against dollar LIBOR and it is prepared to pay dollar LIBOR against a fixed rate of 9.55 percent on deutschemarks.

The counterparties borrow in their respective cash markets-Counterparty A borrows fixed rate deutschemarks and Counterparty B borrows floating-rate dollars- and then enter a swap.

The first figure depicts just that and the initial exchange of notional principals at the commencement of the swap.

The second figure depicts the debt service in the cash markets and exchanges of interest payments on the swap.

The third figure depicts the reexchange of notional principals upon the termination of the swap and the repayment of the cash market borrowings.

Fig. 1: *Currency Swap with Cash Market transactions (Initial borrowing and exchange of notional principals)*

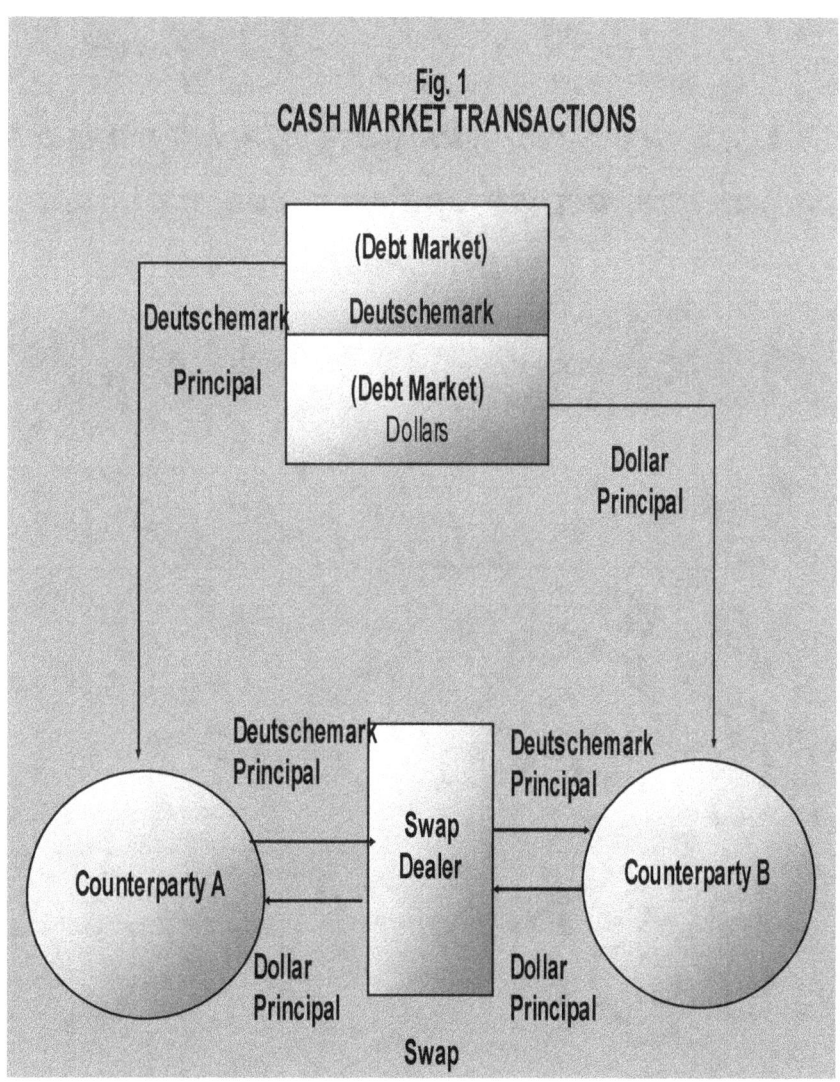

Fig. 2: *Currency Swap with Cash Market transactions (Debt service with swap payments)*

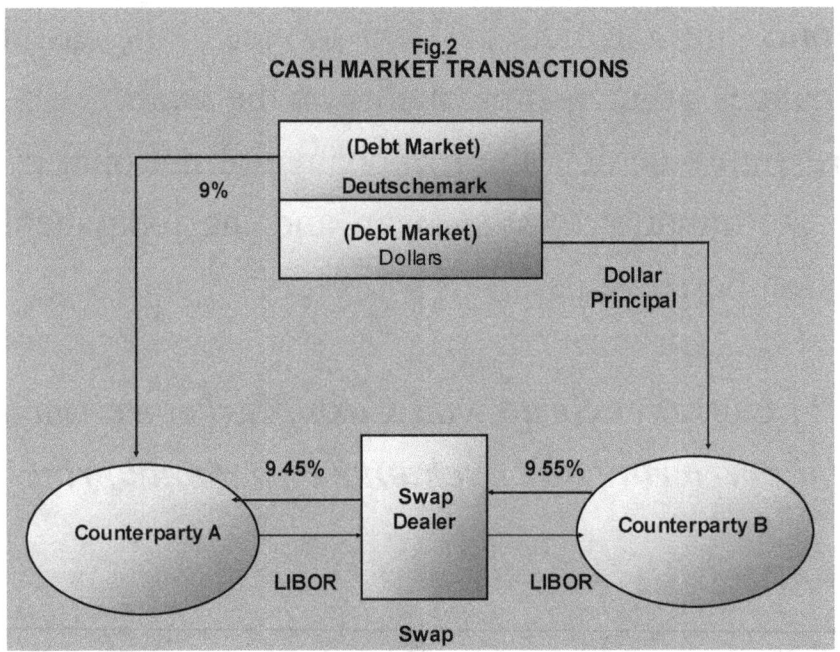

Fig. 3: *Currency Swap with Cash Market transactions (Repayment of actuals and reexchange of notional principals)*

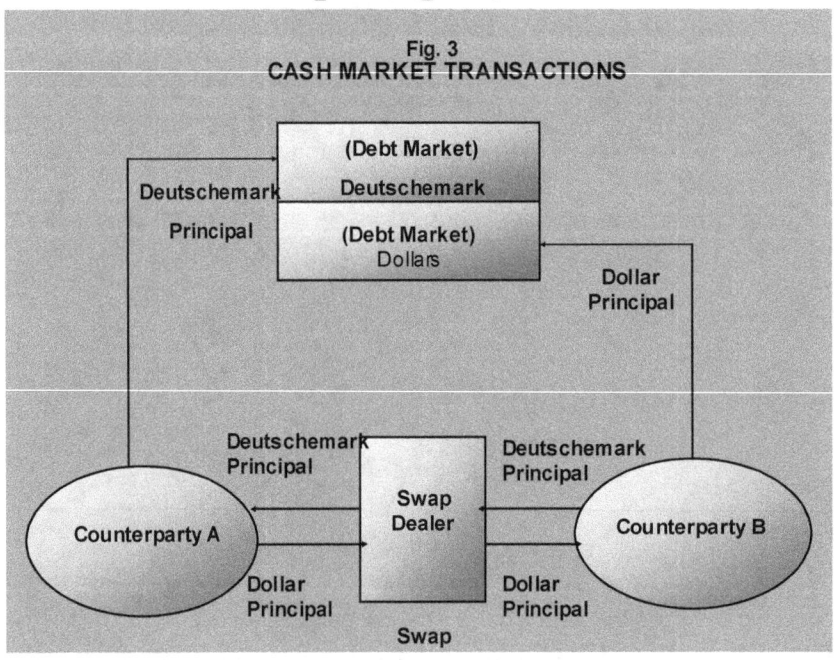

Notice that while Counterparty A borrows deutschemarks, the swap converts the deutschemarks to dollars. Notice also that these dollars have a floating-rate character with a net cost of approximately LIBOR–45 bps. This represents a 45 bps savings over a direct borrowing of floating rate. Similarly, Counterparty B borrows dollars but uses the swap to convert the dollars to deutschemarks. These deutschemarks have a net cost of 9.55 percent. This represents a 55 bps savings over a direct borrowing of fixed-rate deutschemarks. Thus, we see that a swap can be used with the appropriate cash market transactions to convert both the currency denomination of a financing and the character of the interest cost.

The plain vanilla currency swap described above is often called an **exchange of borrowings**. The reason for this terminology is readily evident from an examination of the cash flow diagrams. In particular, examine the first figure. Notice that each counterparty to the swap borrows funds in its respective market and then "exchanges" those borrowings for the borrowings of the other party-hence the name.